Meet Me...
Don't Delete Me!

Internet Dating: I've Made All the Mistakes
So You Don't Have To!

Bev Bacon

Slapstick Publications ◆ Los Angeles

Meet Me…Don't Delete Me!
Internet Dating: I've Made All the Mistakes So You Don't Have To!

For information, contact:
Slapstick Publications
P.O. Box 1012
Burbank, CA 91507-1012

ISBN 0-9744345-8-2
Library of Congress Control Number: 2003097368

Cover and Interior Design: Lisa Liddy, The Printed Page, Phoenix, AZ
Production Editor: Cliff Carle
All Photographs by Yours Truly—Bev Bacon Photography
Visit us at www. bevbacon.com

Names and any identifying characteristics have been changed to protect the privacy of all individuals.

Disclaimer:

The information contained in this book is from personal experience and personal research conducted by the author. No guarantees are made resulting from the information in this book.

This book is dedicated to my ex-boyfriend.
Had he not met his new little honey at
that blasted hot tub party, I never
would have started Internet dating!

Table of Contents

Okay, some people have no sense of humor so here's the real...

Table of Contents

Acknowledgments

Gosh, there are so many people to thank; I don't know where to begin. But since I do have to begin, let's start with Barbara and Frank Jarvis. These two people are the ones who truly created me, made me who I am today, molded and shaped me in every sense of the word. Thanks Mom and Dad, I obviously couldn't have done this without you.

I can't count the hours they listened to every whiny, pathetic sob story about my relationship woes. (At least I think they were listening.) They supported me, comforted me, encouraged me, supplied me with Kleenex, and even after all that, they *still* invite me over to visit.

The other main shoulders I have leaned on are those of my siblings, (and their spouses) Randy, (Sam Soon) Joy, (Dirk) and Janet (Mike). Now that's true love for a sister when they drop everything they're doing to listen to me just one more time about one more breakup. They are my best friends; I love them all very much. And since I don't have any children that I took time away from to write this book, I will brag about my nieces and nephews, Shannon, Keri, Shaun, Dustin, Daniel, Darren, and Kim. You mean the world to me.

A few other very special people in my life who have been there every step of the way are Marie Staddon, Pat Niles, Debbie Sims, and the person who put a fire under my tush to get this book done, David Toma.

A special thanks to my grade school teachers, Miss O'Neal, Mrs. Mullins, Mrs. Tucker, Miss Carens, Mrs. Willoughby, Mrs. Pryor, and Mrs. Zaremski. Without their help, I wouldn't even know how to spell let alone write a book. (I even forgive those of you who sent me out in the hall when I got into trouble, usually for talking.)

Also, a big thank you to Cliff Carle, a very talented man, who pulled this whole thing together with his incredible editing skills. He didn't even need to look at his Caller ID to know when it would be me calling. A line Cliff has heard probably one time too many, "Oh, by the way, just *one* more thing." Thank you so very much.

How can I not thank all the great people who did such a terrific job in the photographs. Your talent definitely poured through making this book so much more special. I'm grateful to each and every one.

Just a few more to thank, the real stars of this book, all of my Internet dates: Allen, Art, Arnie, Archie, Albert, Aaron, Alex, Andrew, Anthony, Alvin, Alec, Andy, Brad, Bill, Brian, Brock, Barry, Brett, Bob, Ben, Bernie, Bruce, Brandon, Brent, Blake, Charles, Cal, Chris, Carl, Chad, Carlos, Craig, Carter, David, Dennis, Darryl, Dick, Dwight, Doug, Don, Dylan, Dirk, Dan, Ed, Erwin, Ezekiel, Ezra, Ernie, Eric, Elijah, Frank, Fred, Francis, Felix, Fabio (I can dream, can't I?) Gene, Grant, George, Guy, Greg, Gary, Glen, Guido, Harry, Hal, Hank, Henry, Herman, Harpo, Howard, Harvey, Herb, Ira, Isaac, Ian, John, Jerry, Jason, Jim, Joe, Jack, Jeff, Jesse, Jay, Jacob, Joel, Jose, Kent, Kam, Kurt, Kermit, Kyle, Keith, Kevin, Ken, Larry, Lon, Lance, Les, Lorenzo, Lamar, Leo, Lloyd, Louis, Maurice, Mike, Mark, Mitch, Matt, Mario, Milt, Mac, Nick, Nate, Neil, Norm, Nigel, Ned, Opie, Orville, Oscar, Oliver, Omar, Otis, Otto, Phil, Paul, Peter, Patrick, Pablo, Porky, Quasi, Queanu (so I'm getting desperate here, leave me alone, I'm on a roll.) Randy, Raymond, Robert, Ralph, Rocky, Ryan, Rodney, Rex, Ron, Richard, Rick, Roger, Roy, Rob, Steve, Sam, Simon, Stuart, Stan, Stimpy, Scott, Sean, Tom, Trevor, Tim, Thad, Tony, Ted, Terry, Ulysses, Victor, Vince, Valentino, Val, Vaughn, Virgil, William, Warren, Wally, Wilfred, Walter, Wayne, Wolfgang, when it comes to the "x"s, isn't that what this book is all about! Then there's Yanni, Yul, Yahoo, Zachary, and finally Zeb.

Okay, maybe I didn't go out with all the above, but after ump-teen years of dating, it sure seems like it!

Thanks a million, y'all.

Introduction

Internet dating is one of the hottest and most popular topics when it comes to the dating scene these days. You can't even stand in line to the ladies room without overhearing someone mention an online date they had or a date one of their friends went on. Even with all the skeptics out there, Internet dating has broken through as a mainstream way of finding the "love of your life." (Or if not that, maybe just a casual friend, new bowling partner, or workout buddy.)

Meeting people can be somewhat of a challenge if you don't enjoy going to bars, getting involved with co-workers, and not having to depend on the "good intentions" of friends and family members to set you up. So what options are left?

The Internet is an incredible tool for giving us whatever information we want on literally every topic in the world at a speed that was inconceivable even a few years ago. (Well, that is unless you still have dial up service, then just forget about anything relating to speed. Grab a book, or two, while you wait for Mr. Computer to catch up with the current clothing fads.) So instead of going out one night a week, hoping to snag Mr. or Mrs. Right, we can sit comfortably in the privacy of our own home and look for a date 24/7. We don't even have to fix our hair, mess with our makeup, wash the car, or if you're a single parent, hire a babysitter.

The Internet not only saves us a ton of time in looking for a date, but can also put us in contact with literally millions of people from all around the world. (This could be good for the airline, car rental, and dog kennel businesses, as well!) We also have the availability of listing the qualities we are looking for to narrow down our search so we won't have to waste time with all the "goobers" and "gooberettes" out there. In other words we can be as picky as we darn well please!

The Internet has been labeled by some as having a "bad" reputation for being unsafe and for introducing us to a lot of lunatics. I don't know about you, but I sure have run into my share of nutcases in person! Those of you who have had your interest piqued by online dating but haven't taken the plunge yet, maybe it's because you've let your fear of the "unknown" prevent you from gathering information on a topic that could have a major impact on your personal relationship. Hopefully, much of what is written will help put your mind at ease about online dating. And for those of you who are currently signed up with matchmaker service(s), I'm sure your chances of success will increase if you read *and* pay attention to the material in this book. (Or if anything, at least let you know you're not alone when you do have a date from hell!)

Oh yeah, let's not forget the "image" thing here as well. I've heard so many people say, "I don't have to find dates *that* way, I would only do that as a last resort." What do you mean "*that*" way? What, you think only freaks from the circus join matchmaker sites? Just ask around, you'll be shocked to find out who's Internet dating. That may have been the prevailing attitude five, maybe two years ago, but currently there are fewer skeptics, and a lot of former holdouts are now converts.

Included throughout this book are helpful tips on topics such as how to find the different sites, how to post an ad, what kinds of pictures to use, what to say, and what not to say when responding to ads, where and when to meet, plus, lots more.

As you read through the chapters, you will occasionally see a "red flag," advising you to pay very close attention—kind of like a little warning sign, or the silent sound of your mother's voice screaming in your ears. (Actually, it's not really a red *colored* flag, just an illustration of a flag, like this:

The printer wanted, not only an arm and a leg to make them red; they also wanted my first-born child, along with the family Pinto station wagon to boot!) Also, each chapter has been summarized with "Bev's Suggestions" for a quick review of the highlights on that particular topic.

I included for your enjoyment, my own personal experiences of dating online just to let you know that I, too, went through all the ups and downs. **I've made all of the mistakes in the process so *you* don't have to!**

This book not only is meant to give advice and suggestions on Internet dating, but to entertain, and give you some laughs along the way. (Mostly at my expense, none the less!) It is my hope that you immediately get going with Internet dating so you can have a blast meeting some new, fun and exciting people. And I want to hear about your own experiences. Please contact me at bev@bevbacon.com to share your best stories, especially the funny ones.

So get off that couch, turn on your computer, and start your travels down the super information highway to finding your "perfect" soul mate!

"Eve, wha-da-ya-mean you're holding out for a better offer? From *who*?"

1 In The Beginning...

If Only Adam and Eve Had It This Easy!

It's late Thursday night. I'm home sitting in front of my computer wearing an oversized white t-shirt and undies. My hair is wet from just being washed and set in my big ol' plastic rollers, and I have absolutely no make up on. I'm sipping on a nice glass of red wine, and believe it or not, I'm actually looking for a date.

Sound bizarre? Not really. Not with the "budding" Internet dating world catapulting us to new heights. Now in the olden days of dating, if I were to try to go out on a Friday night looking like I just described, the only guys that would be escorting me out for the evening would be the men in white coats! Who would have ever dreamed that in today's world we could sit down in the comfort of our house, apartment, dorm room, van, or wherever it may be that we reside, and hunt for a date.

Do you have *any* idea how convenient the computer has made dating? Now I said convenient, not necessarily better. Talk about a time saver and a money saver. Jeepers, we just eliminated one third of the part of our lives that it took to get ready and decide where to go in the hopes of meeting someone, simply by striking a few keys on the keyboard.

In addition, our high tech means of dating can be used efficiently 24/7. We don't have to wait until the weekend, we don't have to wait until we get home from our business trip, and for some, you don't even have to wait until your divorce is final. We now have the capability of looking for anyone, anywhere, at anytime we want. Neat, huh?

Remember the countless hours we spent dolling ourselves up just to spend one evening out on the town in hopes of impressing at least one available person? Hour after hour after hour. Could even be days for some, depending on how cute the person was. I'm afraid to even start calculating the time we've spent fixing our hair, fudging with our makeup and doing our nails. It's almost nauseating. Besides, how many guys have you actually heard say, "Wow! I love your glittery, fuchsia nail polish. It really brings out the veins in your hands."

The most stressful part of getting ready is trying to decide what in the world to wear. What an ordeal! I know I would have *at least* 67% of my wardrobe scattered about the bed as I tried to figure out what combination of blouses, skirts and shoes would make me the hottest thing since Madonna. Come on ladies, you know what I mean. Have you ever left the house where you could actually see your bedspread?

All this time and energy used in hopes of turning a few heads. The sad thing is that all women have to do is wear a low-cut top, a short skirt, and buy the guy a beer. They'll be eating out of our hands all night long!

Let's reflect on some of our favorite ways of meeting people the "old-fashioned" way. Our scavenger hunt would usually start out with sheer excitement and joy, but could, unfortunately, slowly turn into one of those Tylenol moments. Of course the bar and nightclub scene was and still is a hot place to try to meet someone for a potential relationship or a "meaningful" one-night stand. But we all know how most of those end up. It's usually a very short relationship where you go home with someone and do whatever, then you wake up the next morning having absolutely no idea what this person's name is that you are cuddled up next to. Or in rare instances, the one night stand *could* turn into a long-term relationship or even a marriage, whereupon you sometimes *wished* you didn't know his or her name and *wished* he or she would leave when they did wake up in the morning! Scary either way, if you ask me.

Before Internet dating, church functions, health clubs, bookstores, coffee shops, sporting events and even family reunions (Okay, maybe not family reunions. Bad idea.) have been suggested as potential meeting grounds. Oh, and let's not forget good old hot tub parties. But "grocery stores" is my favorite. C'mon, has anyone ever really met his or her spouse in a grocery store? Please let me know. If I ever go out looking like a worn-out slob with cooties, it's when I'm running out to pick up a gallon of milk and a carton of eggs.

Then of course we have our infamous office romances. Years ago, it was common for people to start relationships with co-workers. Why? First of all, you have a lot in common, like your work for instance, and second, the hours you keep are usually similar. Besides that, it's a heck of a lot easier spying on their every little move they make throughout the day.

People are warned all the time about dating co-workers. After all, people may get hurt in the end, then they're stuck seeing each other every day. Dating someone you work with may not be the problem; it's the breaking up part that can create sort of a hellish eternal nightmare.

I think office romances were more popular years ago, but thanks to the current era of sexual harassment, it puts a big damper on interoffice dating. I know guys who won't even *talk* to women they work with, let alone flirt or ask them out. I'm sure a lot of the wives are glad about that. But if you still do choose this route in pursuing a relationship with a co-worker, or heaven forbid your boss, remember, "Hell hath no fury like a co-worker scorned."

How about that all-time *favorite,* the blind date. God bless our friends and families who feel such an overwhelming need to fulfill the void in our lives by setting us up with any breathing, neurotic, post-Neanderthalish person they can scrounge up. Why can't they *stand* it if we aren't seeing someone? Why do they assume we're not happy if we aren't in a relationship? And why do family members freak out if we go two months without a date? The gossip then starts about whether we're gay or lesbian if we go *three* months without a date. Then we have to go into this long explanation about how we're really not, and that we've been trying real hard but just haven't found the right person yet.

Blind dates should be called "blind, deaf, and dumb dates," because that's what you need to be to tolerate most of them!

I hope I didn't bring back too many bad memories for some of you. Now I'm not saying the above scenarios are bad ways to meet people, I'm just saying the Internet is a *better* way to meet people. We can now meet up with people we never would have had the opportunity to before, people who may work in unrelated fields, people who live in different zip codes, and those people with great personalities who we never used to be fixed up with by all the Aunt Ednas in the world.

Even though Internet dating has indeed become the one of the fastest growing ways to meet people, you still have your skeptics out there. Friends used to give me a hard time when I told them I was meeting guys on the Internet. They would constantly chide me, "Bev, I never thought *you* would have to resort to *that* way of meeting people." Or, "Oh, I would never do that, it's too unsafe, and there's a lot of lunatics out there." Gee, I've never met a lunatic out in public before, have you?

What? Did the government develop a new scientific program where "people cloners" make up a brand new breed of humanoids who are born-again cyber beings? And what, these people you meet on the Internet are supposed to be different than the ones we meet at church, on golf courses, and at weddings? Give me a break, will ya! All the people you contact online existed long before the computer; it was just a little tougher to find them is all.

There's a certain degree of safety, or I should say, "peace of mind" when you actually meet someone in person. People you meet just happen to have faces, and you feel more comfortable with that. Is it necessarily safer to go home with a guy or girl you just met in a bar just because you met *in* person? Can you tell if he or she is a drug addict, a sex offender, or married, just because you met face to face? I'm willing to admit I can't. So maybe we should hire one of those psychic hotline babes to chaperone us on our dates, what do ya think?

Well, like anything else in life, we have our success stories and we have our not-so-successful stories. Online dating simply allows us to do an incredible amount of screening before we even meet the person. If any red flags come up in the process, we can *comfortably* end the inquiry and move on to the next person because there's no emotional involvement at this point.

Additional benefits are the countless hours saved not having to get all dressed up to go out on a handful of dates—and for you guys, not having to dump tons of cash on expensive restaurants and what have you. Internet dating also allows us to make contact with a huge number of people, where we can go through the experience, at least in the beginning, in the privacy of our own home!

But what will make the Internet dating experience the most productive and the most enjoyable for you is learning the real secrets of how to meet people online, learning how to qualify them as real or phony, and training yourself how to minimize the potential embarrassments if you finally do decide to meet. Sure there are mistakes to avoid. That's where I come in. (I promise I will try not to sound like your mother!) Between my own extensive experience online and those of the people I ended up coaching, I think we have made nearly every mistake that can possibly be made. I know the terrain. I know the traps. In hindsight, I've learned to laugh at some of the foolish things I've done, and I'm glad to offer you advice on how to make your own forays into the jungle of Internet dating safer, more productive, and by golly, more fun!

So, if you're ready to expand your social life and/or jumpstart your "loooove" life, turn off the tube, grab a soft drink, a cold brewski, or a nice glass of wine, crank up your computer and let's get started down our dot-com world of dating.

" Wow! She's really hot.
I can't wait to see her again!"

"He's my type, he's my age,
he's my dream, and once again,
he's *flat broke*!"

2 A Hard Man Is Good to Find... I Mean a Good Man Is Hard to Find

Finding That Needle in a Haystack

I currently live in Los Angeles, California; the land of the freeways and the home of the plastic surgeons. But I grew up in Kettering, Ohio, right on the outskirts of Dayton. It's not a real small town but definitely not a major metropolis. So trying to find a match made in Heaven was about as easy as finding the golf ball that Alan Shepard hit on the moon.

Almost everyone I met was either married, engaged, under the age of seventeen, or in the process of looking for a retirement villa. Finding someone who was compatible, charming, cute *and* available was not only difficult, but was turning into a full-time job. (With no *bennies*, I might add.)

When I did finally hunt down a willing participant, I would most likely hang on to him whether I felt he was the right guy or not, simply because it could be decades before a replacement might come be-bopping along.

I have discovered that people have such a fear of being alone that sometimes they settle for anyone who happens to be in the right place at the right time—versus finding a more suitable match, you know, like Anna Nicole did. Sounds silly, but I know I've been guilty of it on more than one occasion. (Sorry guys!)

I think I'm safe in saying that most people don't like being alone. Many stay with the wrong person even though they know they aren't happy. Breaking up is terribly hard to do, and no one wants to hurt anyone, and no one wants to get hurt, but sometimes it's for the best.

I look back on every breakup I've experienced. I would sit in my mauve colored rocking chair in my living room for hours trying to figure out why things didn't work out, and praying that I wouldn't end up being the neighborhood's crazy, old cat lady. I would be in a catatonic state for days, sometimes weeks, balling my eyes out because no one loved me. Now that I am older and wiser, I know two things for sure. One, it wasn't my entire fault! And two, I know I hate the color mauve!

Looking back, these were some pretty pathetic times. I somehow seemed to turn each breakup into a major event. I'm sure mom and dad will attest to this. They would sit and listen to me cry for hours over a guy I wasn't even in love with. Time and time again I would stop by their place with tissue box in hand, telling them that my idiot boyfriend didn't want to be with me any longer. It got to the point when I would call mom, just by the way I said, "Hi Mom," voice quivering ever so slightly, measuring a mere 18.3 on the Richter scale, she would say, "How dare he! Come on over, honey, and tell us all about it." Then she would put her hand over the mouthpiece and holler to my father to start taping the Walton's—it's gonna be a long night. I suspect they also kept a supply of Valium on hand for these little incidences, not for me but for them!

At times like these, it felt like my world was going to end. In addition to the pain, I had to deal with the mental picture of the "now ex" frolicking with some bimbo who wasn't half as funny or half as intelligent as me. I would be so mad because I just knew he was out having a blast, and I was sitting home boo-hooing. And each time I wondered if I would ever find true happiness again.

But things are a lot different today. Now, after a relationship ends, instead of going to my mauve-colored rocking chair, I go to the spiffy chair in front of my computer and start my manhunt all over again. Because I now know that there are thousands, maybe millions of cool guys just waiting to meet me. I know because they all say so. It's right there on my monitor. "Pick me! Pick me! I really DO look like this! I DO like long walks on the beach and cuddling. Honest!"

Computers have become more popular than newspaper ads and personal dating services ever were. Dad and mom were more excited about my Internet dating than I was, for obvious reasons. I sold my stock in Kleenex as well.

It's like my mourning period for getting over someone has pretty much diminished, because now *I'm* the one who's meeting someone new and better right away. After my wonderful boyfriend dumped me for Hot Tub Cindy, (you know, the one this book is dedicated to) that's when I decided to jump on the dot-com love machine. I had so much fun going through the personal ads that I almost forgot about...what was his name again?

Even the younger kids don't have far to go to find dates anymore. School was probably the main source of finding boyfriends and girlfriends, (I almost specified "high" school but more like junior high and elementary school these days.) but now even they have access to the Internet. Boy, I wish the Internet had been around when I was in high school. I had to walk five miles in eight inches of snow to take a note over to Billy's best friend so he could give it to Billy, explaining how I thought he was cute and that I wanted to go out with him.

Speaking of high school, (a little background for ya) I realized after my very first date that the journey down Lovers' Lane was going to be a very long, rough and rocky one. I sure didn't waste much time figuring out how traumatic dating was going to be.

I had the biggest crush on this gorgeous blonde boy, who along with myself, was on the school's gymnastic team. He just melted my heart every time I saw him do his floor routine or dismount off the horse. I'm not sure what it was about him that caught my attention; his poise, his grace or those tight, little uniforms the team had to wear, but I was totally smitten.

I was unaware if he ever noticed me, but word must have gotten around that I liked him because a month later he asked me out. I was ecstatic when he called, especially since I considered myself very average looking. Little ol' me, plain Jane. I was skinny, wore very little, if no makeup, and I had a hairstyle and wardrobe that you could find in any National Geographic magazine.

We seemed to hit it off okay, but we never got past the second date, even though I thought we had a ton of stuff in common. Actually, we had too much in common. Quickly I found out that I wasn't the *only* one of us who was attracted to guys. Great! Just my luck, more competition!

I can't think of too many situations that could be worse than that for a person's very first date, although one story does come to mind. When my nephew was in the sixth grade, he received not one, but two phone messages from a girl he knew from school. She called to let him know that she was dumping him. The funny thing was, he didn't even know they were going out! He said he saw her in the halls and would say "Hi," but that was about the extent of their relationship. After the message ended, with a confused look on his face, he asked his mother, "What the heck does it mean to get dumped?"

Getting dumped before you even go out, now there's a newsflash!

My luck with dating in high school only seemed to get worse as the years went by. I went out with a total of three guys on an average of three dates apiece. Let's see, three years, that's thirty-six months, twelve dates, mmm...that averages out to four dates a year. Wow! I bet Mother Teresa would be proud of me.

I don't even want to discuss my college days. Okay, I will, since it will take all of two minutes. For my dignity, I am going to make this as short and painless as possible. I am probably the only coed in the United States, or the world as far as that goes, who went four years of college without having sex. (I think mom and dad were the only ones that felt good about that extraordinary accomplishment!) I had a few, "Would you like to join me in the cafeteria for lunch?"

invites, and a couple guys stopped by my dorm room to get notes from classes they skipped, (Can I count that as a date, please?) but that's about it.

Maybe I made the mistake of going to college in the wonderful "Sunshine State." Not from an academic standpoint (Florida State University was very good to me in that category), but when it came to my female dating competition, the odds were against me. Holy mackerel, maybe I should have thought more about transferring from my college in Kentucky. Girls were known to dress much more conservatively there, compared to attending a college which was packed with more attractive, bikini-clad women than anywhere east of the Mississippi. What the heck was I thinking? I have to admit I did graduate with a fairly decent GPA, though. (I also learned that students with darker tans had a tendency of having lower GPAs than those of the "white-as-snow" students. Go figure.)

Gee, I could hardly wait to see what happened when I went back home and started a real life. Could it possibly get any worse? (Don't answer that!) If you were to graph the number of my dates in high school followed by those in college, the plots on the graph would resemble someone "flat lining" on the operating table. Should I have been in therapy or something? Probably the only way I could have dated any less is if I were in a coma!

Why am I telling you all this? One, it's called venting. This was a horrendous experience that I've kept bottled up for years and I simply wanted to get it off my damn chest. And two, I finally came to the conclusion that the traditional means of dating just wasn't working for me. But Internet dating has miraculously changed all that. With the availability of so many more prospects, not only do I have less time in between dates, my screening process saves me a lot of time and a lot of aspirin. The fact is that Internet dating has made meeting people a lot easier for a lot of people than any other method of dating.

At its inception, Internet dating was outside of a lot of people's comfort zones. I remember when I first sat down and brought up some personal ads, I felt totally degraded. Was I not good enough to meet people in person that I have to resort to this? Was this my only alternative for meeting my future stud muffin? Well, I figured, it beats the sleazy meat market scene now, doesn't it?

What about all the lunatics and socially inept people wandering around out there? Shouldn't we be worried about them? Well, unfortunately, they are out there, but you'll soon learn how to weed out as many of them as possible.

If you think about it, how many good ways are there to meet people? If you don't like hanging out in smoked-filled bars with a lot of annoying drunks, and you don't get laid where you get paid, and if you have your groceries delivered, it's tough to meet people. We all want to meet the love of our life and the creation of the Internet, thanks to Al Gore, (Yeah, right!), has been able to expand our ability to meet people we never would have met any other way.

People sometimes have a tendency to be negative about new things, especially unfamiliar topics. If you aren't willing to open yourself up to new ideas, you might as well live in a cocoon. Alone, I might add.

I have met some great guys who were well educated, who came from great families, and who were clear of criminal records, addictions, and tons of baggage. So don't hold out as a matter of pride, because you'll be astounded at who's doing Internet dating these days. Gird up your loins (whatever that means and wherever they are) and get ready to have fun—lots of fun—exploring the wonderful world of online dating. Even if you've been dating online without success, remember, take heart, you're not alone. I'm here to guide you through it.

As a reminder, throughout rest of the chapters, you will notice the red flag icon, which will indicate a warning that will greatly assist you with eliminating headaches in the future. Also, at the end of each chapter, you will find "Bev's Suggestions," that summarize the key points. From here on out, Bev's Suggestions will simply be referred to as B.S., for short.

For example: The First Bit of B.S.

How do you know that's it's okay to Internet date?

1. When you read studies that show forty million other people are currently doing it, then something must be going right.
2. When, after months of not having a date, you drive not only yourself but also friends and family members crazy with all your whining about not having anyone to go out with.
3. When all of your single friends are too busy on Internet dates to bum around with you.
4. When you start shopping for "Depends" instead of thong undies.
5. When your mom is going out on more dates than you.

Remember: Everything Ventured, Everything Gained!

"So, Dave, you say I should try Internet dating? But who's gonna want a scrawny, buzz-cut guy with lots of tattoos?"

"You know Julie, I really dig scrawny, buzz-cut guys with LOTS of tattoos, but where do I find one?"

3 Don't Give Up! Sign Up!

Deciding to Take the "Net" Plunge

So you're sick and tired of not having anyone to go out with. Poor baby, get over it. Ah, but you can't. Believe me, I know the feeling. The club scene and blind date routine are a big waste of time and you're simply going to go nuts if you spend one more Saturday night alone. So now you're gung-ho about beginning your mission to find the person of your dreams, whether it's your Prince Charming or your little Cinderella, whichever applies to your particular situation. (Maybe both. Who knows, I'm not here to judge.)

Women, maybe you're saying to yourselves, "I've been waiting so long for my fairy tale romance to begin. I'm so tired of being alone; I want someone to share my life with. I'm at the point in my life where I'm asking myself, "Why do laundry for one when I can do it for two just as easy? And it's just a waste of time cleaning up my small clutter, so if I'm going to clean at all, I might as well clean the mess of two people to make it worth my while. God knows I'm getting tired of talking to myself all the time, I would much rather have a man around to nag and control. And why have that big ol' bed to sleep in alone when I can rock myself to sleep by the vibration of my soul mate's snoring. Now where's that marriage license bureau?"

Guys might be saying, "Gee, I don't want to be a lonely old man, I want someone to grow old with, too. I'm tired of coming home to a quiet, peaceful home. I can't wait to be greeted at the door with a list of things that need to be finished before I sit down at the dinner table. And look at all that money I'll save by not going to all the baseball, football and basketball games. (Okay, and all those terrific wet T-shirt contests) I won't even have to succumb to all that secondhand smoke at those all-night poker games. And why spend all that time going on those silly fishing and camping trips when I can be home enjoying the yard I just mowed. My life is here with my sweetheart forever."

So, you're probably wondering, what *can* you do to triple the chances of making your storybook romance come true? Well, you need to do what every other hungry, red-blooded single human is doing, right? What is it? Internet dating, of course. There's no other choice left but to subscribe to a great matchmaker service today. Where do I sign?

Even if you're already doing it (Internet dating, you sex maniacs!), you can probably use some fine-tuning on writing better ads or posting more appropriate photos.

When I first started Internet dating, there weren't many sites to choose from. Well, either that, or my computer ignorance prevented me from finding them. Today there are matchmaker sites for every human characteristic imaginable. And I mean everything! After finding the appropriate site that's for you, with all the lists of goodies to choose from, it's like going into a restaurant and placing your very own specific order. "I'd like one tall, single, wealthy, professional Jewish, Libra male to go."

Nowadays, the computer can't make it any easier for us to find someone to match up with. Now if it could only tell us what to do when we *do* land our match, then yes, we'd have it made. These sites can have a major time saving impact by helping to weed out the person who may not be right for us. Nothing like dating someone for two months to find out he's a Scorpio and not the Leo you always wanted.

You know right up front (because of the long list of questions they ask in your profile) every single, intricate detail that you need to know about a person, that is, unless, of course, they're not telling the truth, the whole truth, and nothing but the truth, so help them Bill Gates. But the good news is, most people who have been Internet dating for any length of time have discovered that fudging with the truth works heavily against them. (Gee, how surprising!) Telling the truth gets you matched up quicker to a person who is looking for your type. (You know, the honest type.) And believe me, there's more out there looking for that type than you ever could imagine.

Some typical beginning questions are: How does one go about looking for matchmaker sites? What kinds are there? How will I know which one is for me? How will I know if I qualify to be in a certain site? (If you're a human being, you qualify. Trust me.) Well funny you should ask. I am here to guide you.

In searching the different sites, I came across one for just about every situation humanly imaginable, ranging from religious sites to sites for millionaires. If you look hard enough, you will find one that will be just right for you. If you believe you're in a category there isn't a site for, you would have to belong to another species besides human. You need to keep searching or focus on some aspect about your life to *make* yourself fit into one.

Start off by typing "Internet dating," "online dating," or "matchmaker sites" in any of the search engines. Here's a few sites that I pulled up when I did a search. Let's start with sites for the different religious groups, which are plentiful. There are Jewish sites, Latter Day Saint sites, Christian sites, Catholic sites, and of course, Atheist sites. (Do Atheist sites really fall under religious affiliations?) I guess some people gave up on the concept of actually meeting at church. I know I did. I would go to every "singles" functions my church ever sponsored, and with every one I went to, the people were already paired up. Discouraged because I did think that these were "singles" functions, there was little left for me to do but attempt to break up those happy little couples. Oh give me a break, will ya? I'm just kidding.

The only religion I didn't find a site for was Jehovah's Witnesses. I was baffled at first as to why they didn't have one, but I came to the conclusion that they probably believe in doing things the old-fashioned way, going door to door.

When I lived out in the country with ten feet of snow on the ground, I couldn't get a pizza deliveryman to come to my house, even if I offered to triple his tip. But would that slow down our JW buddies? They still came knocking on my door at 8:00 p.m., but did they even *think* to bring a pizza? Nosirree, Bob!

I found numerous sites for different cultures as well. They include Indian, Asian, Russian, Latino, Canadian, Eastern European, and if you look deep enough, it wouldn't surprise me if there is a "Red Neck" site somewhere out there in them thar hills. You never know. If anything, this is definitely International teamwork. In what other arena do you find the entire world working together on "togetherness?" Think about it; one big, melting love-pot.

Sites are even broken down socioeconomically. There are sites for millionaires, professionals, and I actually saw a sight for highly intelligent people. (Gee, where does that leave the remaining 98% of the population?) I guess this is an easy way to narrow the search for that money tree that some of you ladies are constantly looking for, doesn't it?

Now you would think, if there are professional sites, it would only be fair that they also have *unprofessional* sites. This could be for all the athletes who never made it up from the farm team. Or what about all the CEO's who get laid off or demoted. We don't want to leave them out. What about pimps, hookers, and thieves? Where do they belong? Lawyers, what should we do with them? Bad question. Never mind.

How about a site for homeless people and bums? Half of them walk around with cell phones, I'm sure they can access the Internet somehow. They could meet at a mutual cardboard box somewhere in town, in a well-lit area of course, and catch up on world events together. I highly recommend no candle lit dinners, however. You know, cardboard and fire, not a good combination.

Other miscellaneous sites I came across were military, gay and lesbian sites, a site for blacks, big and beautiful women, a site for "swingers," college students, (like there's not enough horny coeds running around campus already. Heck, just check out all the "College Kids Gone Wild" videos), single parents, senior citizens, deaf sites, "newly" sober sites, and for those blessed by the stars, astrological sites.

Gee, seeing "astrological sites" brought back ancient history. Has the old pick-up line, "What's your sign?" really come back from the dead? That old conversation starter still comes up more often than I care to admit. I have seen where people do look for specific signs on their profiles, I certainly believe in astrology. I have always gotten along better with certain signs that were more compatible with me; namely, "Curves Ahead," "Danger, High Voltage!" and "Slippery When Wet."

I saved the best for last. I actually saw a site that was for "Positive Singles." Silly me, I thought it was a site for optimists looking to get together, you know, to see the wine glass half full. I couldn't have been more wrong. I was a tad bit shocked when I learned that this site is for people who tested "positive" for things. You know, the things that you don't mention to mom and dad. Yeah, venereal type things and HIV type thingies. Yup, that would be it.

If you run across any sites that make reference to anything concerning "pens," the "big house," state, county, or federally funded "free housing with three free square meals a day" programs, you may want to delete and move on.

I guess it cuts down on embarrassing conversations about diseases before considering having sex. I'll bet most of the people in this site are upfront and honest. I mean, who else would admit to having a disease if the other person didn't have it too, right? So I say, you go girls and boys! Let the good (and safe) times roll.

The sites I listed were more specialized to help you look for very specific qualities in a person. There are numerous sites that are very general that you can "mix and match" the different characteristics you want in your little "heartthrob." So as you can see, there are plenty of sites for everyone. (And I only listed a smidgen of them. Whatever a *smidgen* is.) There is a site just for you, so keep browsing. (Even though I haven't spotted a site for test tube babies and cloned humans, I'm sure one will be coming to your computer soon. It's probably in the works as I write.)

Another thing that is growing fast is what is referred to as "speed dating" or outings where there's a group of people who get together and literally play "musical chairs" in order to meet a bunch of people at one time. These are all fine, but I personally like to start out slow. Let's work on how to meet one person at a time, and then when we become "pros" at it, we can tackle an entire group!

So now you know what's out there. You finally decide on a particular Web site (or change from one you were currently using) and you make the decision of a lifetime to join. (Note: There are numerous sites that offer a short free trial period so you can become familiar with their site before joining. Plus the majority of sites allow you to browse for free.) That's great, so now what? Do you place an advertisement hawking your wares or should you just respond to those people who have already placed a personal ad?

Based on my research, I've found that most people play it safe at first when Internet dating. They post an ad, sit back and wait for the responses to start filtering in. Not me. I believe in being on the offense and the defense simultaneously.

My decision to Internet date was made for me when my boyfriend decided to leave me. No more sitting around whining about what he's doing and me just sitting home alone. Nosirree. You better believe I'm going to be making up for lost time. And boy, did I! Not only did I post ads (Offense), I responded to ads. (Defense)

Remember, "A good offense is a good defense." I don't know who first said that but I like it!

Initially, I simply answered ads. I wasn't crazy about the idea of having my picture up there for everyone and their horny seventy-five-year old grandfather to drool over. I felt answering ads was the best way to go. I could be selective and only answer those that I was truly interested in.

But I know so many women who would never respond to a guy's ad. It's the same thing as not approaching a guy in person. Why not, I would ask? "Well, if they're interested in me, they will approach me." Some women feel the same way about answering guys' ads. They feel like *they* are chasing the guy and it's not a lady-like thing to do. I assure you that is antiquated thinking.

Many guys are unable to read the "signals" a girl sends that say, "I'm curious about you. (And, "Will you buy me a drink?") Guys can be shy too, you know. Are there any laws stating that the men have to be the ones making the first move? They have enough pressure on them already, don't you think? Or should we ladies just set them up so they can experience a higher risk of rejection? I don't think so.

Most of the guys I dated in the past came as a result of me going up to them. So, I think it's time for a change. Ladies, unite! Get over this idea ingrained in our society that we aren't permitted to approach a guy and initiate a conversation. It's not like you're asking him to jump in the sack or anything. Quit feeling sorry for yourself if you continuously go home without a phone number or sit home on a Friday night because you chose not to answer a guy's ad, simply because you feel you have to follow ancient protocol. Lighten up a little. That way maybe you won't be boo-hooing all weekend!

I know guys *love* to be approached. How do I know? I know because I've asked them. They're usually flattered and it's nice that they don't *always* have to make the first move.

If you're still hesitant, put your ad up first and let them chase you. After a while, if you're not getting the results you want, start answering their ads. Keep in mind the "good offense is a good defense" slogan. There is no right or wrong approach, this is a two way street by my experience.

I've met some great guys by responding to their ads. Even though sometimes nothing long term came from it, it sure beat sitting around the house talking to myself all night long. It's always fun to meet new people and hear about their lifestyles and experiences. Even if you don't hit it off romantically, try to gain something positive from each date. (I almost used the word *meeting*. These are not meetings you go on, they're dates, even the first one, as far as that goes.) One source I read about Internet dating stated that you should not consider the first "get together" as a first date. It should be considered date zero. Could someone with an IQ of seven or higher explain a "date zero?" If it's not a date, it should just be zero. (Nothing!)

You may get tips on a new restaurant in town, or learn about a new tennis club to join, or find out about a great museum. Think of each outing as a good experience. If, with all the positivity you can muster, you still feel it was a bad experience, turn it into a funny story to tell your buds at your next party. Plus, it's comforting to know that the other person is struggling to meet people as well, and that you're not alone here.

Finally, both responding *and* answering ads can only double your chances of going out. It's kind of like being bisexual, waaaaay more opportunities!

More B.S.
(I don't have to remind you what that stands for now, do I?)

1. The best way to find the different matchmaker sites is to type in "Internet dating," "matchmaker sites," or "online dating" in the search engines.
2. A number of sites have a short free trial service. If you are unsure which service to use, check out the freebies first. If you're feeling lucky, then you can sign up for a month membership.
3. By both posting an ad and answering ads, you increase your chances of getting responses.
4. If you're hesitant about your first attempt, invite a few friends over and make a party out of it. (However, if you start fighting over the same ads at your party, you may want to try it solo for a while!)

P.S. If, after looking over all the sites and none seem to pique your interest, I guess we'll be seeing you in the meat section of your local grocery store!

Strict Monogamist Looking For Same

4 A Picture Only A Mother Could Love...Well Maybe

Deciding Which Photo to Post

Whether you've had an ad up for awhile or are brand new at this, if you're like most people, you may want, or need, a little guidance on how to begin your journey or how to repave the road you're already been down. Before going off on any excursion, it's always nice to know how to get where it is you need to go. Most people wouldn't go on a trip without having a roadmap of some sort to point them in the right direction, so why not arm yourself for this adventure as well. (For you males out there, a roadmap is something that is generally found in the glove box folded up a million times which can be instrumental in helping you find certain destinations.)

You've finally admitted to having a problem: not being able to find a mate. Recognizing this is the most difficult step to overcome in our "Thirteen Step" program, or however many steps it takes to get you on the right track. Could be as few as three, or as many as 20 for you perfectionists out there. But now you have to take the next step: Putting your mug on the market for everyone to see. (And judge!) In doing this, you are definitely on your way to stepping outside of your comfort zone in hopes of finding that wonderful, perfect soul mate.

The thought of having your picture on the World Wide Web for every friend, relative, co-worker and enemy to see can be a little intimidating at first. Okay, maybe not a little intimidating, maybe anxiety producing on the level of going to a proctologist...with big hands. So deciding which photograph to use will probably be the most critical step in this process. Due to subject matter, this may not be a topic to get mom and dad's advice on. Since they're not in the picture, (pardon the pun) I, a complete stranger—kind of like on the same level as a sage bartender—will throw out a few recommendations. Well, actually more than a few. After all, this is an important section.

If I'm not mistaken, I do believe that most people have the same objective I have when placing an ad; we want to meet someone. No matter how much we hate to admit it, there has to be some level of attraction before any type of relationship can begin.

Do you realize that companies and corporations spend millions of dollars on advertising to best illustrate the product or service they are selling? Image is everything in advertising. So what are we doing? We're *selling* ourselves, aren't we? (Not literally, ladies!) Thus, we need to represent ourselves the best we can for our viewing audience.

I have to admit, I have scanned my share of ads over the years. And I must say, I've been highly entertained along the way. Some of the photos I've seen could make a guy's own mother turn over in her grave. I'd like to know what in the hell some of these people were thinking when they chose the particular photo they did to "advertise" themselves to the entire universe.

Now remember, probably 97 percent of the people are going to respond to an ad based on what they see in this photo. We could boast that we won the Pulitzer Peace Prize for finding a cure for cancer, or that we were able to balance the national budget on our home calculator. But if we post a picture that looks like a bad clone of Charles Manson, Lyle Lovett, and Marilyn Manson combined, people won't have any more incentive to answer your ad than if you were an eighty-year-old pregnant woman with Herpes. (Which I am sure there is a Web site for.) If you *should* happen to look like a cross between the gents listed above, at least smile pretty, because a smile can go a long way.

One thing I've frequently noticed is a large number of photos that are out of focus. Now I know everyone's not a photographer, and you may not be able to afford to have a professional headshot taken, but by golly, tell whomever is taking your picture to please take their nerve medication first!

Maybe subconsciously the guy is thinking we won't notice the wrinkles and bad teeth if the shot is blurred. I'll bet a few drinks might help it appear sharper; it's worth a shot. (Pardon that pun, too!) But when you go to meet the guy, I guess it would be a good idea to have a couple of belts in you so he will, indeed, look like the same person who's in the photo.

Also, there are times when size *is* important. (I'm talking about the photo in this particular instance—what'd ya *think* I was referring to?) You may want to consider using an image size that's larger than a single brain cell of an ant. It would be to your advantage if viewers could tell what species you belong to. Example: what's with the picture of you water skiing behind your friend's boat, splashing water twenty feet into the air, 350 yards offshore? I guess if we never got closer than 350 yards when we meet, we won't have a problem now, will we?

A nice shot from the waist up would be nice, including all the way to the top of your head. Speaking of which, I saw an ad where this guy had posted not one, not two, not three, but four photos of himself with the top of his head cut off. What does this mean? Can I use him as an end table and put a bowl of chips and a drink up there, or is it possible he's just a *hair* uptight about being bald? Hmmm?

Look, we'll find out sooner or later that you now have the same amount of hair that you were born with, so get real, get a clue, or look up the nearest toupee dealer in your area. Just let it go. Besides, there are a lot of women who find the male balding pattern kind of sexy, except for that combed over flippy thingie going on. Like it or not, this is part of who you are, and I know it is very difficult for guys to deal with, but c'mon, it's much better than some of the other hair options guys use to deny reality.

Another point I would like to make is if you post a photo with your ad; make sure we can see certain key elements, like your face. What's up with photos where the guy's wearing a ball cap and sunglasses standing in the shadows where all we see is his shady silhouette? Why take the time to post a photo when your audience can't even see what you look like? This being the case, why don't you just turn around, bend over and snap a shot of your backside instead, what would be the difference?

As I mentioned earlier, I know we may not be able to afford to have a professional portrait taken, but you still have several options. Instead of using any old snapshot lying around, take a few minutes to click off a new one. This will be everyone's first and possibly last impression of you. If you don't have access to a camera, don't hesitate to ask a good friend if you could borrow their digital camera or cell phone (is technology great or what!) to take a pleasing photo. As an incentive, tell them you will pass down your overflow of dates.

I know some people have extremely busy schedules, and others are just too damn lazy to have a new picture taken, but posting your driver's license photo on a matchmaker Web site to attract your next potential spouse! Crime-a-netly, (as my grandmother, bless her soul, always used to say) who do you plan on attracting, one of the slow moving clerks at the Department of Motor Vehicles? Why don't you just post your mug shot from your last arrest instead, it would be just as impressive.

I kid you not. I have seen several pictures with the State of California written across the top in that neat heliogram stuff. Nice touch. If anything, at least we know you're old enough to drive.

Other interesting photos I've seen floating around in cyber space include one of a guy standing in the bathroom donning only a towel wrapped securely (thank goodness) around his waist. Another guy took a self-portrait of himself standing in front of a mirror;

you can actually see him holding the camera in the reflection. Boy, this guy must be a blast to hang around if he doesn't even have a buddy to take a photo of him. Come to think of it, I'm not sure I would want to go out with *anyone* who feels the only place he feels comfortable having a picture taken is in the bathroom. Would you?

I really love the ones (yes, plural) where the guy mentions that he's the life of the party but his photo looks like he's a poster child for Preparation H. In another photo, if I didn't know better, I would've thought the guy just got home really late from a killer bachelor party. If he wasn't drunk, he really needed to find a better Laundromat.

This is definitely one of my favorites. Please, someone help me understand why a guy would include a photo of himself standing next to some 25-year-old blonde (a female, not a lab or retriever). Or worse yet, a photo with half of a 25-year-old blonde visible! Are we to assume this is your adoptive daughter, or your niece, or maybe it's the pool girl? Or are we suppose to think you're just plain loony?

By seeing you with a beautiful woman, are you trying to make us jealous, or are you trying to makes us believe that you can get really hot chicks even if you look like a creature from *The Night of the Living Dead* movie? What gives? I would go out with the driver's license guy before I went out with the guy with his ex in the shot. Now even if it isn't your ex in the shot, you must know how the female mind works. We will believe it *is* your ex, or current fling, unless a twelve-member jury can prove beyond a reasonable doubt that it is, indeed, your sister.

I realize that some people can't stand to be alone, but can you have at least one decent photo of just yourself so we don't wear ourselves out speculating on who the mystery lady is? Geeeesh.

I saw one picture that not only included the entire 20-something blonde, but she was wrapping her arms around a 45ish-year-old guy in a big bear hug. (Great incentive for luring in potential dates. Bonehead.) Now I shouldn't jump to any conclusions, I mean with all these so-called "blended" families or guys marrying women half their age (Oh, yes, this does happen) maybe that was his new step-mom. I seriously doubt it. I think the guy's just a clueless jerk.

Another photo had a guy sitting in a rocking chair holding a baby. Not bad so far. But what caught my eye was the blonde leaning over the chair doting on *both* of her infants. (Notice the other woman is always a blonde? Hmmm.) Are these guys advertising for a threesome? Did this photo get mixed up with the one that's to adorn the Christmas card photo? In Heaven's name, what should I think of this? Maybe he's looking for a baby sitter. All I know is that my brain is hurting from trying to figure all this stuff out.

After glancing through a few more, I realized I could write an entire book on photos alone. What do you do when there are two guys in one photo? Are they too cheap to get their own ad? Is this a package deal? Could it be their way of coming out of the closet? Now Siamese twins are a whole different matter, but as far as I could see, these guys weren't attached anywhere except for the single brain they both seemed to share.

One more then I will have said my piece. I know this computer age thing can be complicated and if you don't know much about it, it can be a pain in the butt. However, one thing you should learn, is how to post a photo that has not been stretched out like Gumby. I saw one where I thought the guy was the center for a pro basketball team, but on closer inspection I realized the photo had simply been distorted. I think he was actually 5'5" but was trying to give us the illusion that he really didn't fall "short" in the height department. Another one looked liked the guy was really an anorexic stick figure. Again, on close examination, it was just a squooshed, unnatural pixelie thing going on.

So, if you are unsure how to use the computer, scanner, digital camera, and yes, the cell phone, do what everyone else does, call the nearest five-year old to help!

Note: If the person has more dots on his face than a box of dominos, don't delete him/her right away. He may not have the chicken pox or a bad case of acne. It could be that the photo was scanned at a very low resolution. (Like 4, maybe 5 dpi)

All right, all right. I have picked on the men's photos long enough, but it was so much fun. However, I can't let the women get off that easy here, either.

I haven't spent a ton of time flipping through ladies' ads, for obvious reasons, but for the purpose of research and, okay, to check out my competition, I did my fair share.

Most of the photos that women put up actually impressed me. But then again I guess that wasn't a total surprise. The majority of women do try to look their best, (as I'm sure you guys can attest to, as you sit in the living room watching all three sequels of the "Terminator" waiting for your date to do her hair, makeup and wardrobe thingie), so I'm assuming that they carry the "getting ready" part over into their photos.

In general, (either in photos *or* in person) women are probably more concerned about their appearance than men. Or actually, now that I think about it, maybe it's because we *can* do more to improve our looks. Guys are pretty much stuck with what they have, to a point. I'm sure we would look twice if a guy wore concealer for those nasty blemishes or eyeliner to accentuate his eyes. Hair options are really limited and I probably would pull a red flag out of my hat if the guy had "pumps" on to help in the height department. I guess that's why they have nice cars to impress us with, huh?

I did happen to notice there were a slew of shots including the kids. I can't sit here and tell you not to include your children in your photo, but the first thing that comes to mind is that the guy might think he's probably going to take a back seat to your kids. You will list in your profile that you have kids, so let them see just *you* at first glance. The guy might love kids and it's not a problem that you have them, but guys are visual and when they see three people in the photo, they envision three people *all* the time. If you want to include the little rug rats in your photo, put them on the second page of your ad instead.

Speaking of our lovely visual creatures, a.k.a. men, no matter how shallow it may seem, guys are, and most likely always will be visual. If you have a nice body, don't hesitate showing it off a little. That doesn't mean showing a wide, gaping cleavage shot, or wearing a string bikini. But let them see first hand how all that hard work at the gym has paid off! (Speaking of bikinis, if you elect to wear one in your photo, my only comment is, you better *still* look like that when you meet the guy.)

In the first photo I posted on my site, I wore a blouse that was a little tight. I thought it might increase the chances of getting guys to respond. Well, it did that all right, along with increasing the number of drooling sex maniacs that responded. I learned I could get just as many responses with my charming, witty personality as I could by wearing a tight, low cut top.

Guys like to see more than just your face. If you don't like how you look, don't worry about it, they may not mind.

But if you *really* don't like how you look, dress according to your size for a more pleasing look. In other words, if you're a size 14, don't squeeze into a size 8 hoping to "impress" the guys. Yes, it's a known fact that the average person carries a few extra pounds. Either accept it, or do something about it. Just don't try to lie about it.

Of all the guys I have spoken with, the "most popular" complaint I hear is that women never look like their photo. It wasn't exactly taken yesterday, more like "50 pounds ago." Misrepresenting yourself will get you absolutely nowhere, and it says more about you than hiding a few pounds. How can you benefit by putting up a photo that doesn't look like you? Do you really think they won't notice when you finally meet later on?

As I mentioned earlier, covering up who you are is only going to let the other person down. Yes, weight is probably one of the biggest...or I should say, main reasons why men may not answer an ad. I don't want to sound mean or cold, but that's the sad truth, in a nutshell. On the other hand, there are pa-lenty of guys who don't mind a woman with a little extra weight, and there are some guys who actually look for plus-size women. So, you decide how you want to handle things from here on out, straightforward, or not so straightforward. If you want this thing to work, you have to work with it! DON'T be deceptive!

Do not, I repeat, do not lie or cover up anything about your looks. People can get around a few extra pounds much easier than they can the lying.

One friend of mine mentioned to me that she wasn't getting many responses from her ad and I had a difficult time figuring out why, her being an attractive brunette and all, so I started asking questions to see what her strategy was. The first thing I asked her was what photo she used. She said she posted a photo of her standing next to her aunt. After scratching my head in disbelief, I asked, "Why did you choose a photo that included your aunt?" She quipped, "Because I love her." Unless you're advertising for a *ménage a trios*, I'd stick to having *just* you in the photo. Guys might think that the other woman is the owner of the brothel down the street, or worse yet, what you might look like without makeup! Who knows how the male mind works, it sure baffles me at times.

Here's another major concern when addressing the issue of photos, how recent is it? You would think the average person, with an average IQ of, let's say 50, would automatically post a picture that was taken within the last 12 months, you know, to let their potential prospects know what they truly look like. Well, that was my thought initially too, but noooooooo. We have to continually make things more difficult, don't we?

A friend of mine told me that when he went to meet his date for the first time; he thought the woman who greeted him was his date's mother. The woman had apparently posted her high school graduation picture, ASSUMING he wouldn't notice the twenty-five year age gap. And she thought that photo would work? What could she have possibly been thinking? (Thinking being the key word here.)

The only way I would post my high school graduation picture is if I were trying to impress someone who spends the majority of their time at the local Braille institute.

What cracks me up is when guys get tired of women misrepresenting themselves, but then they turn around and post a ten-year-old photo. Guys always asked me how recent my photo is, but I never thought to ask a guy that question. I mean what man lies about his age? After numerous occasions of having the guy look like Patrick Swayze in his photo and looking like Patrick Stewart (referring to the hairline here) in person, I finally asked if his photo had been taken since the last Halley's Comet. (By the way, when asked how old photos were, the average response was five years ago. Geesh, babies aren't the only ones that change over time. Get with the program here, folks!)

Eliminate most surprise elements of a first date by posting a photo that shows how you currently look. That way the date will have a much higher probability of going smoothly.

When I was commenting about how attractive this one guy's photo was, he said, "Oh yeah, that's the one where I still had hair." Alrightythen.

Okay, so I'm back to talking about men's pictures when I was supposed to be talking about the women's photos. Am I getting graded here? Then I see no problem, do you?

Anyhow, this particular case is a rarity when it comes to the age of photos, but one guy posted photos that were seven years old, and the only way I knew was when he told me. I never would have guessed that this man had not changed significantly over that length of time. I begged him to tell me where he was hiding the fountain of youth. Besides that he had a body that could force many of the Chippendales into early retirement.

No real reason or significance for that example except for the fact he was soooo cute. (Still is.) Oh, now you're wondering what happened with this guy. People tell me I have a habit of not finishing stories, complete hogwash; I don't believe I do that at all.

Okay, back to women's pictures once again. You should be aware of another complaint I hear quite often from men. It's when they see a really hot chick, I mean *really* hot, nine out of ten times, they're directed to go to the woman's personal web page. It usually turns out that the "hottie" is offering some sort of service where money is exchanged, specifically his money going to her. I think this is sad, and I think it turns off most guys. (At least the money part.) Even if guys *are* out there just to get laid, they don't want to give out credit card numbers. There's already too many sites designed specifically for those services, (Besides, guys know that sooner or later credit cards are going to be a BIG part in any relationship he has with a woman, right?) I'm sure in some cases these personal Web site scams work, but I feel they only pollute the personal ads and gives the rest of us sweet, caring, loving girls a bad name.

Be aware of ads that send you to a person's private Web site. Credit cards are usually involved, along with other stuff your mom and dad probably wouldn't be too proud of.

What about posting sleazy shots? Short and simple, you get what you advertise for. Case closed.

The bottom line is that we're trying to meet someone to spend time with, right? Then why in the hell are we submitting photos that wouldn't even land us last place at the annual dog show? You don't have to be model material to submit a nice, pleasing photo. And I really can't understand why someone would go through this entire process of Internet dating just to slap up a really bad, blurred, dark, unidentifiable photo.

It's a shame we put so much emphasis on picking out the best photos, verses the best narratives of the ads when three-fourths of the time, the people don't even remotely resemble their picture. I highly suggest reading more of the ad before making a hasty decision based solely on a picture.

It's really pretty simple. Just post a photo of you, and just you, that we can see, that's fairly close up, in focus, pixelie corrected, not including every member of your family tree, that was taken at least twenty-four hours after your last hangover, leaving out any member of the opposite sex, and that was taken within the last six months. And for Pete sake, smile!

There are no laws saying that you have to smile. And even if you aren't a smiley type of person, try using a photo with a look that somewhat resembles a smile, like a "hint" of a smile. (Even smirks can work in some cases.) If you represent yourself as being unhappy and miserable, that's your decision, just don't get upset when your response level is lower than you expected. Be cautious: If a guy/woman has five photos posted and he/she is not smiling in any of them, it only leads us to believe that they either have hemorrhoids or they have no teeth! (When I use he/she, I am speaking in both gender cases, not about transsexuals.)

Remember, positive attracts positive, or something like that. So say cheese and act like you mean it, by gosh!

Photogenic B.S.

1. Don't dig through high school yearbooks for your personal ad photo. (That is unless you graduated in the last week or so.) Post a photo that was taken within the last six to twelve months.

2. Glamour shots are outdated. Try finding a photo where only half a can of hair spray was used.

3. With all the fancy digital gadgets we have now to take and manipulate photos, I highly recommend against major reconstructive surgery by retouching out every single, wrinkle, blemish, scar, and mole. If this type of photo is already posted, then you best make plans on taking a couple of hits of Botox on the way to meeting your date.

4. Smiles add a nice touch!
5. Wear something with a tad bit of taste in your photo, especially if it's full length. Leave the worn out Rolling Stones t-shirt in the closet. (Or better yet, at the Goodwill store) Great! I'm going to get yelled at now. So for all you die-hard Stones fans, I'll substitute the raggedy t-shirt with one of Motley Crue.
6. Use a close-up head and shoulders photo for the front page of your ad. If you include additional photos, use more of a full-length or waist-up shot. For the second page (yes, some of the sites have up to five pages) you can also be adventurous and use the ones taken with Fido, and Mittens, and of course, the young 'uns.
7. For all of you Einstein clones, think twice about using shots of you on your snow skis (and snow suits and snow hats and snow mittens and snow goggles). We can't tell if you're a he or a she or a snowman or Bigfoot. Move in closer!
8. Make sure we can see your…FACE!
9. Leave out grandmas and aunts and cousins and ex's and former girlfriends, current girlfriends, nephews and pool boys from your photos. STAND ALONE!
10. If you post a photo that makes you look like a Playboy Bunny, you better have Hugh baby in the background.
11. If you're going to include your Mercedes, Porsche, or Harley in your photo, make sure that it's nice and shiny.
12. Don't be afraid to switch photos occasionally. If one doesn't work, try one with different clothes or a different hairstyle, or a different expression.

Conservative Church Going Gal
Looking For Match Made In Heaven

5 Rocket Scientist Looking For Pet Project/Cute Gemini Will Double Your Fun

What Headline to Use

How many times have you gone out and seen someone that you were attracted to? You're dying to go up to him or her but your brain goes AWOL and takes your vocal cords with it? You know you only have a second to react because he/she will probably be leaving soon, but you can't think of a dad-gum thing to say. By the time you do coordinate your body movements with your mouth movements the person is long gone, or your fear-of-rejection factor has kicked in. Nine times out of ten, you end up walking away with your mouth open knowing that you let another opportunity go right down the drain.

I don't care if you're in church, on a golf course, taking a night class or at a night club, knowing how to approach someone can be more difficult and more frightening than running into Jack Kevorkian at your neighborhood block party (or anywhere as far as that goes!). I can't count the times I saw some cute guy but didn't do anything about it. Not because I was afraid of rejection, God only knows how used to that I was, but in my ability to speak the English language in a manner that another human—preferably—male would understand. Whatever the case may be, I just couldn't think of anything to say quick enough. I mean what do you say when you see some gorgeous hunk in the frozen food section at the grocery store, "So, what brings you here?"

Once again, the computer eliminates that gawd-awful feeling of awkwardness. It buys you time to figure it out. By posting an ad we have all the time in the world to figure out what to say to get someone's attention. There's even a place for it: the initial contact line. I'll refer to it as the headline, or the "Hey baby, what's your sign?" line.

These headlines are basically human advertising tag lines. They're used to catch your eye and (hopefully) reel you in. You only have a handful of words to sell yourself so you'll want to take a few minutes to come up with something catchy.

To me, the headline that a person chooses can, to some extent, be indicative of his or her personality. Besides the photo, this is the next thing people see, so a defining statement needs to be made. Even though there's only room for a half dozen words, be creative and fun here.

Not only do you have to decide on a headline, you also have to come up with a code name in order to keep your identity temporarily anonymous. Most people will simply choose a nickname, which is then followed by a series of numbers, like surferdude758. Why there's a series of numbers after a code name is beyond me, but as the nice policeman always says, "I don't make the laws, I just enforce them."

Always start out using an anonymous email account, which does not reveal your name. Give out your real name only after you have emailed back and forth a couple of times and feel reasonably comfortable with the person.

Going through ads and reading the headlines can be as much fun, if not more than going to the local comedy club. This line is kind of like the first impression, (or second impression if you check out the photo first), so you'd think people would want to make it as appealing as possible, yet they often provide some pretty profound "scratch your head and mutter, what in the world were they thinking?" moments.

I do have to wonder what goes through the minds of some of these people when they decide on a headline. I'm sure a lot of them are nervous and have little experience, but I swear they must have had a few too many "brewskis" before they sat down and put on their little thinking caps.

I will bypass reading certain ads due to the content of the headline. "Lonely Single Dad of Five Seeks Woman" just didn't set off fireworks for me. I'm not quite sure why. "Fathr of Too Brite Childrn Lookn for Companyon" didn't get me all hot and bothered either. (Have you ever heard of spell check, guys?)

"I've got Herpes Simplex." No, I'm not divulging my personal medical history—this was actually a title I saw on one guy's ad. He went on to say that he wanted to be upfront and honest, that half the population has it, so why not get it out in the open. I give the guy an "A+" for honesty and an "F" for snappy pickup lines.

A lot of guys will put their profession in their headline, such as "Hunky Lawyer Seeks Cinderella," "Tennis Star Looking for Love," "Chiropractor Looking to Crack You Up," and "Cardiologist Willing to Give Heart Away." Catchy! And do you notice any similarities? They all make tons of money.

Have you ever seen "Garbage Man Willing to Sweep You Off Your Feet," or "Bus Boy To Service Your Needs," or how about "Box Boy Looking to Bag a Babe." How many people do you think would answer those ads? Not a whole hell of a lot. There are probably a few gorgeous garbage collectors out there but you may want to hold off mentioning your occupation until somewhere in the narrative part of the ad. We're only human, what can I say?

Again, since these people won't get a glimpse of your charismatic, charming personality until you meet, so use whatever ammunition you can to intrigue someone. Since most guys can't understand the significance of putting up a decent photo, they rely on their profession, especially if it's a good paying one, to lure you in. Plus, it's beneficial to put a high paying profession in your headline because women have no idea at this point what kind of car you drive.

I have to admit, I have responded to a few ads just to find out who the guy is. I answered one that had "nymets" in his headline. I was a tad bit curious, was he affiliated with the New York Mets baseball organization? Maybe he's just a big fan, but why waste time guessing, I wanted to find out.

I can't believe I responded to this ad based on his potential affiliation with the Mets, although I am allowed, and so are you. There are no rules here, folks. If he did play ball for them, it would be totally cool to say I went out with a former major league baseball player. Maybe a friend or my ex-husband, who is a huge baseball fan, will recognize his name and get jealous. My luck he was probably a batboy or a hot dog vendor.

Well, I did end up meeting him. Matt and I met briefly at a nearby park, and it wasn't Shea Stadium, but we only talked for about fifteen minutes, since he said he had to leave for work. I was so glad he was able to squeeze me into his busy schedule; after all we got to know each other *so* well. I hope he didn't think I was too demanding of his time right off the bat.

To make a long story short—actually it's not that long—how long could it be when the entire "date" lasted all of fifteen minutes! (Why would anyone set up a time to get together knowing they only have fifteen minutes? Could someone explain this to me? Inquiring minds want to know.) It turned out he had been on the team as a pitcher for all of two weeks. I guess everyone and his brother, cousin, stepsister and grandma was on the injured list, so they brought him up from the minors. I can't remember why he only got to play for such a short time, but at this point it really isn't an issue anymore, certainly not worth bragging about.

Needless to say that relationship never got to first base. Not because he wasn't well known, but because he called me twice within five minutes to ask what I thought of him. "Well, what did you think? Was I as good looking as my photo? Do you think we'd be a good match? How many kids do you want? Is Hawaii a good place for a honeymoon?" Puh-leeeez.

You won't believe it, but I did it again, I answered an ad that had "gbpackers" in it. Back then I didn't know why I responded, maybe to rule out the fact that anyone who puts a professional sports team in their email isn't necessarily associated with the organization, but simply trying to lure women into answering their ads on false pretenses. Gotta give them credit for trying, it lured me in.

Now I believe Roger, the "gbpackers" guy, told me his name was put on the team roster but he never made it up, not even as the team bench warmer. I also heard where he was recently removed as president of the local Tailgate Party Association due to misleading credentials.

Before having these pieces of crucial data, I met Roger for lunch one afternoon. He seemed like a nice guy...until he opened his mouth. He talked about himself for the first hour, asked me all of one question, and then proceeded to try and recruit me into one of his many multilevel marketing schemes. Terrific, this was just what I needed. I told him I thought I had looked in the personal ads, not the job ads.

Well, if the Internet dating scene is a means for him to grow his MLM business, fine, just don't come within 300 yards of me. If he hopes to meet potential business partners, that's great, but on the first date! Come on, get a life! His headline should have read, "My Way or the Amway."

If you're answering an ad based solely on the fact that he mentions a professional sports team or anything remotely affiliated with a professional organization; check to see what else is in his ad. (When you find out he's only the vice-president of the fan club, you better hope there's some other good reason why you want to meet him.)

A few other laughable headlines I've seen are "Lonely Homely Gent Seeks Someone," "Semi Famous Bachelor Looking for Love,"

"Desperate Man Seeks ANYONE," and my all-time favorite "Rich, Well Endowed Doc seeks Special Lady." Now which one of those guys do you suppose got the most hits? Hint: You can rule out the lonely, homely gent.

Let's go back to the "Semi Famous Bachelor" for a minute. For some unexplainable reason (okay, for research) I actually met up with this guy, again because the headline somehow intrigued me. It turned out that he worked in the finance department for the Philharmonic Orchestra. I just couldn't bring myself to ask him which part of him was semi and which part of him was famous. At least I have my answer to what semi-famous means. (Jack Squat.)

That one didn't last past the first date. Not because he wasn't famous, but because he came across as being extremely insecure. Plus, he tried to hold hands with me on the first date and I can't *stand* that. I guess I feel holding hands with a complete stranger is about as awkward as playing the violin with your fingers. (Gee, no telling what will happen if the guy tries something more than just holding my hand!)

I've come to the conclusion that answering an ad based on what the person does for a living is nothing but a waste of time and money. Yeah, money's nice to have, but when you start spending more and more time with a person, the money, or who they are or used to be doesn't seem so romantic or as genuine for some reason.

Now, let's take a quick look at the award winning performance by the infamous "Rich, Well Endowed Doc." He sure made good use of his four words. You can't get much better than this one. I bet myself that his mailbox was full. Well, actually I know it was, because I responded and there was a message stating that his mailbox was full. I'm only human, what can I say? I never did try to respond to his ad, there were too many other great ads to choose from.

You can't blame guys for letting women know what their profession is and that they make big bucks. It's a solid selling point whether we want to admit we are shallow or not. It's funny but very few women seem to put anything about their occupation in their headlines. I am sure "Cleaning Lady: Just the One to Get the Job Done," or "Girl-Friday Only Available Saturdays" might be on the short end of the stick when it comes to generating responses.

On women's ads, I saw several variations of "Princess seeks Long Term Friend," "Precious Kitten Looking for Studly Dude," and "Goddess Seeks Hunky Hercules." Cute, but what are they trying to get across? I guess they feel putting something cutesy is better than listing a job profession that may not get them a lot of attention. The problem is some men will associate the word "Princess" and "Goddess" with high maintenance. Be careful!

It's tough coming up with something unique and original, but it's necessary if you want to stand out from the competition. But allow me to mention a few that really *wouldn't* be on the top of my list for landing guys. "Lonely Aquarius Seeks Fun Guy," "Marriage Minded Maiden Seeks Love God," "Committed Searching for Soul Mate," and "Mother of Four Seeks Family Oriented Male."

Are these women trying to attract someone or send him to an early grave? Do yourself a favor, never use the words "lonely, commitment, marriage, long term, soul mate" or "mother" in your headline. Don't you know that most guys are allergic to those words, at least in the beginning? Give him time to ask you out before you frighten the buh-geezies out of him. Dating is a process, and it can and should be a slow process at that. It takes time to get to know each other and to learn what both of you are looking for. Find out his last name before you start shopping for wedding rings.

I saw where one gal was seeking a long-term "friend." I hope she was referring to a plutonic female friend because I don't think too many guys would fit that description. Further down in her ad she said she was looking for "just" a friend but also mentioned that she wanted kids. Okay. Well, either she will be satisfied as a step mom, do the adoption thing, or take a shot at the artificial insemination thingie. If she only wants a friendship, someone may have to explain to her that she won't have a whole hell of a lot of kids if she doesn't want anything more than that.

Another gal's headline was "Hourglass Figure," but for some reason she only included a photo of her head. Interesting. Anything hourglass related, I'd be showing off to anyone belonging to the male species.

Here's one that stumped me: "Honest Gal Looking For Fun Dan." Okay, now this is interesting. Is she only looking for guys named Dan? Or maybe it's a typo and she's looking for a Dad. Or could it be she's looking for a Man? How much time are we supposed to spend figuring this one out? Can't anyone reread what he or she wrote just once? You are, in a way, being graded by your readers, so scan over your ad for mistakes before you are mistakenly deleted for not knowing if you want a Dan, man, dad, or cad.

Watch your spelling, people. One little letter can make the difference between a doc and a dog.

"Sophisticated Seeks Rich Guy." Okay, let's quit beating around the bush. What is it that you really want? What qualifies you to get a rich guy? Just because you're sophisticated entitles you to some guy's hard-earned money? I think "Shallow Lazy Gold Digger" would be more apropos, don't ya think?

Now I did see one that was kind of cute. It said, "Let's Watch Sports Together." Now she obviously has done her homework on knowing what guys want. This other girl had a clever one as well, "Hiking Guru Seeks Happy Camper." It's cute and light, nothing heavy.

In my first ad that I posted, I wanted to put "Free Six Pack with Response," but then I figured I wouldn't know if the guy wanted to go out with me or if he just wanted to collect his free gift. I also liked, "I Come With A Big Screen TV." Think women. Think like a guy!

Humor is a concept that is foreign to a lot of women when it comes to trolling for mates. It's a good thing; don't be afraid to use it. It's not illegal to let loose every once in a while. There are so many women out there walking around like their tampon's in crooked.

Lighten up gals. You will see this topic more than once, trust me. (Humor, not tampons.)

Then there's "Looking For a Husband." Gee, did you have to spell it out? I think the word "husband" should be added to my list of banned words, whaddaya think? Most guys probably realize this is your final destination, but let's have a few pit stops in between, alrighty?

Be cute, be original, and stay away from the no-no words.

One of the main conclusions that I have come to is the more adjectives that are used, the more insecure one is. "Successful, Rich, Handsome, Built, Romantic, Studly, Intelligent Brain Surgeon Seeks Female." A little deep, wouldn't you say? He's probably 4'9" weighs in at 234 pounds and has a Michael Jordan hairstyle. And, I'll bet he drives a Ferrari.

These insecure folks are usually the ones who also have the vanity plates that say, "1Actor," "SF 49ERS," or "GR8 DOC." Translation: "I wanna be an actor," "I'm a big fan," and "My urologist is the best."

Here's a perfect example of my above theory:

I saw an ad that was entitled, "Successful Working Actor Wants You." Now there's not a warm-bodied female out there who wouldn't be curious to find out who this guy is. Anyone saying they wouldn't want to go out with someone who even *claims* they're an employed actor is lying. Yup, it caught my attention. I normally wouldn't have answered this ad because of the, "Let's see how many adjectives we can use in one sentence" rule, but because of his headline, Pandora's box flew wide open and my curiosity got the best of me.

Even though he had a photo posted, I didn't recognize him as a television star. Since I don't watch much TV, and when I do it's usually cartoons, I probably wouldn't have recognized him if he was, indeed, a working actor.

Now, when you live in LA, you quickly find out that there are a lot of wannabe's in the entertainment field whom when you ask, "What do you do?" they immediately respond, "Oh, I'm an actor."

So when you rephrase the question to, "Great, well what do you do for a *living?*" the answer's usually something like, "Well, in the evenings I work at the local movie theatre tearing ticket stubs" or "I'm a telemarketer for a phone company." I just wanted to clarify the working status of people who live in LA versus other parts of the world. (Not all, mind you. There are people who actually do say they are "trying" to get in the business. You generate much more respect that way.) In other words, don't get your panties all in a bunch when you see the word "actor" in a headline.

Now where was I? Okay, the photo was nice and even if he weren't a successful actor, I still would have responded. So now I'm past the headline and photo. It only gets better, folks. His physical description was fine, and again, I'm still interested at this point. But when I get down to the narrative where he describes himself in detail, I was turned off quicker than a straight guy in a gay bar.

He only wrote 40 words, but 33 of them were a string of adjectives describing what a hunk he was. "Fit, handsome, generous, confident, intelligent, funny, sensitive, manly," and "assertive" were a few that he mentioned. He did leave out modest, though. But the other things he said made my few remaining brain cells go into a tizzy. He continued by saying that he had a totally ripped hard body—not just a hard body, and not just a ripped hard body, but a *totally* ripped hard body. Then he sprang his award winning ending, stating that he was definitely the "Filet Mignon" of the personal ads. According to whom, his butcher?

First of all, if the guy had a totally ripped hard body, why in the heck did he wear a baggy shirt in his photo? Why did he wear a shirt at all! Women can be visual creatures too, ya know. Secondly, what does "totally ripped" mean?

Giving him the benefit of the doubt that this guy is not the "Filet Mignon" of morons, I couldn't help myself, I had to respond to see what made this guy tick. I wanted to find out if he was who he really claimed to be, or if he was in fact an out-of-work comedian.

I was close to his match profile, but fell slightly short (or slightly long, depending on how you look at it) in the age bracket, but I knew my sense of humor would get him off the fact that I was 16 months older than what he was looking for. So I wrote a cute message telling him I was interested in finding out more about him. And lickety-split, he responded back. At this time, I didn't have an ad posted, so there was no photo for him to see of me right away. His warm, sincere, gentle, passionate response just took my breath away. Verbatim, his first correspondence to me went like this,

> "Send photo and phone number to my email address. Make sure you send photo of body *and* face. Upon receiving photos and number, I will call you and we can meet. Bill."

What is he doing acting? He should be a staff writer for Harlequin romance novels with juicy, hot stuff like that. Can you believe this guy? Not that it's required by law to start off a letter with "Hi, how are ya?" but it makes you feel more like, you know, a "human."

Since my curiosity was still piqued, I decided to go to the next step since I'd already come this far. After all, I won't get the part if I don't audition. I sent Bill a photo showing my body from the thighs up. I was wearing a fairly tight tank top and shorts; you know, to accentuate my totally ripped hard body. I thought that would show him just about everything he needed to see. I didn't send a separate "face" shot because in this particular photo my face was attached to my body, so I figured—or I should say—"assumed" that would suffice.

You'd think. No, he wrote back and told me to send a photo of my entire body. The only things you couldn't see in the first photo were my lower legs and my feet. I again, assumed he could figure out that my lower legs would be somewhat in proportion to my upper legs, maybe even a little smaller as calves tend to be. Okay, cutting him a little slack, maybe he's received similar photos in the past of other women who happened to have had not one, but two prostheses, and he wasn't sure if this is what he wanted.

So even though the guy was confident and secure, and he believed he was the hottest thing since volcano lava, in the end I decided to cut him loose. Even if he really thought he was secure, why did he have to try so hard to convince us by reiterating it a million times in his ad? So instead of landing me, this guy landed in my recycle bin.

If there are more adjectives in a headline than there are words in a dictionary, you may want to consider the level of their insecurity before spending time with them.

Apparently, Bill wasn't getting a lot of responses with the headline he originally used, which was "Successful Working Actor Wants You," because when I saw his ad up months later, he had changed it to "Successful *Hard Bodied* Working Actor Seeks Woman." Okey dokey.

Excuse my reiterating on the subject, but I feel it's a crucial point that the more adjectives a person uses to describe him or herself, the more insecure they are. It's just like having to tell someone that you're being perfectly honest. Why would you have to tell us you're being honest unless you have a reputation for being dishonest?

Let us be the judge if you are ripped, honest, and hot. Keep things simple and life will flow much more smoothly.

Catchy B.S.

1. Leave out words like *lonely*, *commitment*, *abnormal* and *mother* from your headline.
2. Remember, the more adjectives you use to describe yourself, the more insecure you come across.
3. Be funny; humor is always a safe bet.
4. Put a hobby in your headline like, "Snow Skier Seeks Chair Lift Companion" or "Bowler Looking for a Guy With Balls."
5. Think like the other half and put in things that they may enjoy like, "Channel Surfer Seeks Same" or "Seventies Rocker Looking For Seventies Roller."
6. Use positive words and phrases. "Desperate Loner Looking For Any Breathing Soul" will not get the same responses as "Happy Energetic Engineer Wants Brainy Beauty."

"Yeah, I'd definitely call this an athletic build."

6 Five Foot Two, Eyes Of Blue, Let Me Be The One For You...

Describing Yourself for the Entire World to Desire

Okay, you've selected a quality photo, presumably of yourself, or changed an existing photo of bad quality, and you've come up with a catchy headline. Now you get down to the good stuff: The personal profile. Here you are presented with the opportunity to list your personal data in such a way that people will actually want to meet you.

Any site you choose is going to have a personal profile area that will give us a general idea of who you are. Not too much thought should go into this because you should already know the answers and shouldn't have to think of anything flowery to say. These categories are all very cut and dried. All one has to do is to fill in the little blanks. Easy, right? Well, see for yourself.

Usually the first question asks your gender, male or female. Very simple, wouldn't you agree? Well, it used to be to be simple years ago before they started all this sex change stuff, so I suggest if you can't choose male or female, you may be one of those who would want to start your own "Singles" site, such as "Horny Hermaphrodites."

I caution you that this will be a very good time to start using spell check if you haven't already. I was going through ads one evening when I pulled up this gem. If I didn't know better I would have thought the ad I was reading was not a guy's ad but that of a woman's. *He* looked just like a woman, described *himself* to be 5'8",

130, long brunette hair, sexy, funny, loved yoga, crocheting, and dancing as hobbies, and described what *he* thought would be a perfect first date as going to a lovely tea house in Boston. Now I've never claimed to be a brain surgeon but the only thing I could figure out is that either *he* is looking for another guy or instead of putting F for female, *she* put M for male and her ad ended up in the "Male Seeks Female" section. Gosh, I thought we started with the simplest question there is, but thanks people, for the added laughs.

ONE little letter can be detrimental to your ad, so for Pete's sake, or anyone's sake, watch your spelling!

Next on the list is age. Gee, let's get this out in the open and over with right now! Great! This is the one topic we women spend our entire life trying to hide and now we have to announce it to the entire world. And I *know* everybody puts his or her correct age; I'll bet not one soul out there has ever lied about that one. You know why I know? Because before you sign up for a service they have a sixteen-page agreement you must read and agree to before they take your money. There's a "loyalty clause" that states something like, "I promise that I answered all my questions on this matchmaker dating site truthfully and honesty, so help me Guido."

I always knew women lied about their age, but it shocked me when I found out how many guys did, too. I thought guys were more secure than that. Yeah, forty is waaaaay older than thirty-nine. And forty-nine doesn't sound half as bad as fifty! But it cracks me up when I meet a guy and before we even sit down, he lets me know that he fudged his age by a few years. Nice. Now that I know he's a conniving liar, I won't have any surprises later, now will I?

Today's forty-year-old is much younger than the forty-year-old of twenty years ago. But it doesn't help make it any easier for us to tell people we are forty. Again, it bothers us more the fact you lied about it than if you were older and told the truth. If you look younger than your age, we will notice by your photo or when we meet in person. If I was designing a matchmaker Web site, I would have an age range as opposed to having you put up just one little, lonely number. But who am I? I know of a couple sites that now do, in fact, allow you to list an age range, so if you feel you don't want to let people know exactly how old you are, maybe this is the way to go.

How about ethnicity? Again we should all know what we are. Now there are some people who are just pure "muts." (And I mean that in a good way.) They're half Irish, a quarter Asian, an eighth Puerto Rican, and an eighth American Indian. If this is the case, I say it would be okay to put "Other" in this section. Another option could be, "See photo" or "Call mom for verification."

Hair and eyes. Giving this some thought, I realize this isn't going to be that easy either. Hair, that's the little fuzzy, shafty thingies that grow out of your head. Either you have them or you don't. If you do, you generally list what color. On some sites, for you folically challenged people, they have skin-toned as a choice. If that's not politically correct I don't know what the hell is.

Then we have all this hair dye, and highlights and hair extensions, wigs, and Mohawk stuff happening. What if you have a red Mohawk but the shaved sides are blonde. What do you put? I guess some of the sites came up with the "mixed" choice for you creative creatures out there. If you highlight your hair, do you put the most prominent color or the one you want to be most of the time? Do you put "natural" blonde or "it came out of a box" blonde?

I saw a guy's ad where he described himself as being a blonde but also stated he was Jewish. In his photo, he had what appeared to me, and probably the entire sighted population, the dark features of a Jewish man. He had the same hair color in the other four photos as well. So am I missing something here, folks? Is this the case of another typo? Is he a wannabe blonde? Maybe color blind, I really don't know. This is simply wearing me out!

Eyes, that's easy for most. Not for me, though. When people ask what color my eyes are, I go into my, "They're brown around the center and hazel-greenish on the outer edges, and for some reason only God knows about, I have one green contact and one blue contact." So I usually end up putting, "Just look at them when we meet and come to your own conclusion."

Location, a.k.a. where you reside. If you live in a small suburb or a town people may not recognize you may want to list a large city that's close by to give a general idea where you are. I answered several ads from guys who listed that they lived within miles of me, which I thought was fantastic, considering a six mile commute could mean an hour drive in LA. Well, come to find out these bozos put down where they worked. Why? To throw our scent off track if we happen to be stalkers? Either that or maybe they don't want us to run into their wife and three kids playing in the front yard.

Is there just one easy question we can answer? Let's try this one, smoking preference. Translation: Do you smoke or don't you? For most of us this is easy, unless you are one of those people who smoke but don't inhale.

I don't smoke, I don't inhale, and I don't walk around with a pack of cigarettes rolled up in my shirtsleeve, so I put down, "doesn't smoke." Easy enough. I also put that I am looking for a nonsmoker. So what does this one goober do? After our second date he confesses that he does smoke even though he said he didn't on his ad. Well, that clarified things; I just assumed he was wearing his "lady killer" nicotine-based after-shave.

Marking "no answer" on smoking is another Einstein moment (or I should say "Clinton" moment.) What? You pull it out of the pack, light it, put it up to your lips, and then sit there like the Mona Lisa? Or do you only inhale on Thursdays. I know, you only smoke when you go out drinking. How far can you stretch denial, my friend?

When you select "no answer," do you think we're going to *assume* you don't smoke—or that you haven't made up your mind about starting yet? Odds are that you do, in fact, smoke. These are ads I usually delete because if a person isn't big enough to admit he smokes, he's not big enough for me to go out with.

Other general questions can include religion, political views, and education, drinking preference, group affiliations and profession. These are categories that people actually excel in answering, and there's not much to make fun of, so I'll move on.

There are sites that actually ask if you have any body piercings, tattoos or other body art. Jiminy, they're eliminating all the surprise elements, aren't they? We'll know so much about you that we won't even have to meet. And Heaven forbid, a little rose tattoo on your butt may cause someone to delete you immediately (even without getting to know you) if they're not a tattoo kind of person. This certainly could have been a Seinfeld episode unfolding here.

On some sites they ask for an income range. Personally, I feel this is being a little too nosy. Unfortunately, this is something that's also known to be used as bait. Years ago, income was never brought up in conversation on dates, it was considered inappropriate. I know some of the most intimate details about some of my friends' lives but I would never ask them what their income is.

Know this: when someone puts down that they make over $100,000, it doesn't necessarily mean that they really do. You could be answering an ad based on false pretenses. Just keep that in mind when you see those six figures. It goes both ways with men and women. If you want a guy who wants you for your money and not you, go ahead and share your income and wait and see how many times he offers to buy. It shouldn't take you too long to figure it out. That is unless you fall "in loooooove," then you'll be blindsided, he'll take you for everything you have and when you fall off of cloud nine, Mr. Gigolo will already be in Tahiti and you'll be looking for a lawyer and a guest spot on *The Ricki Lake Show*.

If a guy claims he's the CEO of a huge corporation, but you see him hop off a city bus when he comes to meet you, I'd keep my eyes and ears wide open! Just be careful when answering ads based on income. If that's your only agenda, save everyone some time and go straight to the site for millionaires.

Kids. Do you have any or not? If you men are unsure, just list an approximate number with a question mark behind it like, "4(?)". That way we can put you on a sliding scale to see if you are a tad bit of an irresponsible, uncaring jerk or a major blown-out irresponsible uncaring jerk.

You don't have to go into detail if they're your kids, your step kids, your brothers' kids, or whatever. If this becomes too confusing, just list the ones you know you have to pay child support for.

Yep, some guys mark "Other" or "No Answer" in the spot for "Do you have kids?" It sure seems like a black and white question to me. Besides, if you only get to see the guy every other weekend and *never* on Father's Day you know he has at least one kid out there.

So if the guy you're dating makes no claim to having any offspring, and your gut tells you otherwise, sneak a peak in his wallet for photos, or in his house for signs of Barbie dolls or action figure men.

Knowing whether or not someone has children is extremely important to many when deciding to become involved with someone. Be very upfront about this situation. (I have known of cases where this tiny, "insignificant" detail has been left out until later in a relationship with disastrous results.)

Body Type. If only Webster had a good definition for this one, it sure would save us a lot of surprises. Sites usually offer options to choose from so you can't just list any old thing you want. Selections for body type include slim/petite, average, athletic build, slightly overweight, thick, or large. Different sites will use different adjectives, but they all basically have the same meaning.

This is definitely a subjective field. We all think of ourselves a little different than how others perceive us. There's a fine line between slim/petite and average, but there's a big difference between petite and gargantuan, so take a few seconds, stand in front of a mirror and proceed to answer the body type question as honestly as you see fit.

My favorite response is the "athletic build" category. In my mind I see a swimmer, a gymnast, a soccer player or a basketball player. (Sorry bowlers, I can't include you here.) I've met men who have a physique like John Candy to a physique like Tommy Lee who list themselves as having an athletic body. I guess if you were a ballerina or a sumo wrestler, you would, indeed, fit in this category, so I'll leave it up to you to use your better judgment.

I realize it's tough trying to describe yourself, I know it's hard for me as well. But when I'm asked to portray what it is that I look like, I try to downplay a little, rather than exaggerate. If I say I have an average body and guys see me in person, they're going to be a little more surprised when they find out that I do, in fact, have a "totally ripped hard body." Okay, maybe not that, but I do keep in fairly good shape. (I'm also the type of person that if I lost track of my golf score I put one additional stroke instead of opting for the lower score. I know, call me an idiot, but I sleep better at night. After thinking about it, I could probably sleep better with a lower golf score as well. Hmmm.)

Many people probably feel that if they say that they have an athletic body, they will get more responses. But that's not always the deciding factor. If all people only married skinny people, the number of marriages would drastically drop off this side of the planet. (I know, you're going to tell me that your spouse was thin *before* you got married.)

By the way—my lovely readers—may I digress? Is there a clause I don't know about that says you have the legal right to let yourself go to hell in a handbasket after you have "won" your prize? What happened to all those hours of doing the makeup, hair and nail thing? This goes for guys, too; maybe not the makeup and nail thing, but you know what I mean.

It's funny, after your first date, the appearance scale seems to drop drastically. You stop wearing nice shirts and nice shoes, and start opting for the jeans, t-shirt and gym shoe look. That's okay for a casual mid-week get-together, but for a nice Saturday evening out, you may want to dig deep into your closet and scrounge up a nice pair of Dockers and a pair of loafers, that is after removing all the cob webs. If people (that includes you men out there) only realized how good you look when you dress up just *one* little notch, you'd be surprised at the attention you might receive. Jeepers, I really do sound like your mother here, don't I? Well, this is an advice book, and I am only trying to help!

Getting back to body descriptions, one site I visited had choices of average, above average, and very good looks for physical appearance. Needless to say, 90% of the men listed "above average looks" or "very good looks." Now if you could grace the cover of *GQ* magazine, put "very good looks." If you could grace the cover of *Werewolves Weekly*, you may want to jot down "average looks." Again, people read this and have very high hopes. Our definition of "very good looks" can vary, so be modest here folks, it won't hurt you.

As shallow as this may seem, looks play the biggest role in this crazy dating game, so be very objective when describing yourself. A little modesty can go a long way!

Marital Status. Where do I even begin? Choices are fairly black and white here: single, divorced, widowed, separated, and on some sites, "married, but wish I was single." (Okay, I made that last one up, but there's a lot of you who are thinking that!) Depending on what you're looking for, you may want to study this answer carefully. I have been careless on occasion and overlooked this item a few times. Big mistake. So remember what it is that you are looking for and proceed accordingly. This way we can save each other a lot of time and heartache.

If you are looking for a committed long-term relationship, you may want to avoid the married, somewhat married and even the separated ads. If they say they are separated, at what point are they in their separation? I've found that in many cases separation is just a state of mind, not a geographical fact. Often these folks are still living with their soon-to-be ex. According to my *Random House Dictionary*, separation means, "To put or keep apart by an intervening barrier or space." The space between one side of the bed and the other side doesn't qualify if you ask me.

The guys I've met who were separated were at stages varying from, "I'm leaving the house this very weekend," to having been separated for five years, but just haven't got around to doing the paper work. You should go with your gut on this one.

What will happen if you become attached to this "separated" person? Even if they are physically separated, it could take months, if not years, to finalize the divorce. Then there's always some type of adjustment period and maybe a little "I want to play the field" period. The word *rebound* comes to mind at this point, as well. Again, I am not the judge and jury; you'll have to make up your own mind. But please be cautious!

Some people have been known to list that they are legally divorced when they really aren't. How can we tell? Do we hire a private investigator? If you date him for oh, five months and you have never seen where he lives, that might be a clue. How about if you never see him on weekends and holidays, or if he has never introduced you to his kids, or he has never shown an interest in meeting your friends and family. These could be little hints as well.

If the person uses the word "discreet" in their ad, I don't care in what context; move on. Discreet and being available almost never mix.

You don't have to read between the lines to figure this one out. Why would anyone want to be *discreet* if they weren't already in a relationship? Be leery of people who are very secretive or evasive; usually they have good reason to be—or *bad* reason.

One woman told me she had been emailing this guy back and forth for a while, and thought it was strange that he never answered any questions she asked him. He would write back asking her questions, while ignoring all of hers. I told her that he was married and to delete him. She wanted to know how was I so certain. "Experience," I told her. Sure enough she pulls up his ad and under "marital status" he had marked "No Answer." Jeepers, a "No Answer," for "marital status?" How intelligent is that? What's next for this guy, the leading role in the next *Jackass* movie?

There are usually very clear signs of potential problems, yet we often choose to ignore them. Ladies, quit making up excuses for the guy! (Actually, this goes for both genders from here on out. I'm a female, so I usually talk from a female perspective. I don't want you guys thinking that I'm picking just on you.) After six months of dating, if he has never spent one holiday with you, or has never spent one night with you, and you choose to continue to ignore the warning signs, it's time to wake up and smell the coffee, cappuccino, chocolate latte or whatever it is you wake up to each morning. If you're willing to deal with this fine, but quit feeling sorry for yourself and quit whining to your friends and family.

When a person answers a question with a question, changes the subject quickly, or becomes uneasy without provocation, chances are, you've hit a nerve. Dig a little deeper to see if your suspicions are well-founded.

I read this one ad and really liked what I saw. I was anxiously waiting to see if he would respond after I wrote to him. I sent a photo, he approved, and he too, was anxious to meet me as well. Now here's a case where I became lax and didn't read his entire ad. He did list that he was single, but in his narrative he put, "I am interested in having a friendship that could turn into something more, and if you are a single person or have a companion and are looking for something "on the side" drop me a line. I am a *serious* man so only those *seriously* interested need to respond."

I *was* serious so I replied. He wrote back and said, "I may not be what you are looking for. I am married, very happily for 17 years, and my wife gives her approval as to what I am doing, so I may not be the one for you." Okay, does your "I am looking for a friend to possibly turn into something more" mean you are hoping it turns into a threesome? Maybe a golf buddy? What?

You guys can write and say anything you want, but keep in mind what it is that you are truly looking for. Being humble is always good. It's much better to be pleasantly surprised than grossly disappointed on a first date. Because if you are disappointed the second you meet, you won't hear a word they say, and they aren't going to notice how charming and funny you are because in their eyes you were being deceitful.

So if we are truly in the market for a relationship built on trust and honesty, we need to show by example. What's that cute little saying we learned in the second grade, "Honesty is the best Policy." So by gosh, let's work on it a little, can we?

Very personal B.S.

1. Hop in front of a mirror before you select which body type category to put yourself in.
2. Choosing "No Answer" for smoking preference and the number of children you have does not look very impressive in the "intelligence" department. Strike one.
3. When it comes to having children, mark down the number that truly exists. When answering about wanting more, do the same. If you don't want anymore, also say so. Don't try to figure out what the other person *wants* to hear.
4. To keep things simple, put your gender at birth.
5. When you lie about your age, it makes us wonder what else you're willing to lie about. Strike two.
6. Don't forget to list group affiliations and hobbies. This could be a great conversation starter.
7. If you feel it is vital in getting more responses, go ahead and list your income. Otherwise, I recommend keeping hush. There are a lot of people who are anxiously waiting to take advantage of someone with money, especially women. Think twice!
8. Try to put your location as close to where you live instead of where you work, play ball, or like to vacation.
9. Selecting "No Answer" for marital status will not make you the sharpest crayon in the box. Strike three. You're out.

"Maybe I didn't make myself clear when I said, I like a guy who "dresses up" for a date?"

7 Matchmaker, Matchmaker, Make Me A Match

What You Are Looking For in a Mate

Even since childhood, I think we all have, at one time or another, conjured up ideas of what our lifelong sweetheart would be like. I'm sure we have pictures (in focus, close-up and without shades and a ball cap, of course) in our mind of what we would like to have if we could "manufacture" our perfect soul mate. Naturally we want someone who is attractive, intelligent, financially secure, caring, honest, supportive, active, financially secure, compassionate, thoughtful, emotionally stable, spontaneous, romantic, and did I mention, financially secure? Wouldn't this be a lovely world if it were that easy?

Unfortunately, this *is* the real world and it *ain't* that simple. What happened to the days when everyone settled down with his or her high school sweetheart for fifty years? The way things are going with relationship woes today, the only thing that's going to last fifty years are memberships to Internet dating services!

Internet dating gives us the opportunity to literally create exactly what we want, at least on paper. The "match section" is where we get to list every specific trait we want in our partner. The sections here are identical to the ones we answered in our own personal profile section. You mark down what you are looking for as far as age, gender, location, body type, hair/eye color, education, income level, marital status, religion, smoker or not, political and "kid" preference. (Again, the setup can vary from site to site.)

This is also the time and place to weed out all those so-called "undesirables," so take advantage of what you want now so you won't have to whine about it later. When I posted my ad, I was pretty basic, didn't have too many items on my wish list. Basically, if the guy was standing, breathing on his own, and had some cash flow, that would make me pleased as punch.

To eliminate mass decision making on the old noggin, if you're not sure what to put or you simply don't care; just mark "Any" in these blanks. The more popular "Any" categories usually include areas such as hair color, religion, political views, employment status, education, group affiliations and astrological signs.

I marked "Any" for most of the choices on my ad but there were a few areas where I did want to be more specific. Like gender, it was pretty much males only. Sorry ladies, no can do.

Another topic I was specific about was location. Trying to keep it somewhat close to home, I put down a twenty-five mile radius hoping I wasn't narrowing the field too much. For most people, traveling fifty miles is a cakewalk, but in L.A., fifty miles could turn into a half-day road trip. Depending on which direction you go, *ten* miles can be a highway nightmare. I just thought it would be neat to meet someone who lived within three tiny traffic jams of me. Anyone living within one tiny traffic jam would receive one complimentary gift on the first date for not making me face all those mean, angry drivers.

The other categories I was specific on were smoking preference, wanting more children (my eggs are so old I wouldn't be able to *give* them away on ebay) and of course marital status. Pretty important issues when you are trying to find someone to live with happily ever after.

The smoking category should be fairly easy to answer. Either you like breathing in smoke or you don't. Believe it or not, this is a category where most people won't bend. No matter how attractive, how much money he makes, or how fancy his car is, some people just aren't willing to put up with the fumes (*his*, not the car's).

And if having a family is going to be an issue down the road, here's your chance to put up a roadblock before you start investing all that money in family counseling. Kids are very high on the list of priorities. Make sure this subject is agreed upon in the beginning because there is nothing worse than spending three years with someone thinking you will change his mind into wanting kids, or more kids when, in fact, he doesn't.

If kids are in your future, make sure they're in his. If you both are unsure, fine, see how things progress. If you see a studly hunk, and he is everything you want, but he doesn't want kids and your eggs are screaming, "Please release me, let me go…." delete him. Why date four months, then mention the fact you are dying to have kids when you knew going in what the answer was. I know, you *think* you can change his mind.

If a guys puts in his ad that he has no children and does not plan on having kids in the future, hiding the child car seat and the spill-proof cups in the trunk is probably not in your best interest. When it comes to having children, this is a major topic of concern in planning for the future, so don't make this black and white issue a gray one.

Regarding the good ol' biological clock, I would refrain from mentioning anything closely related to that topic on a first date. That is, unless you only want one date per guy. How could you even mention kids to someone you don't even know? Now I know he's probably thinking it would be fun to go through the motions of *making* a baby, but most likely it won't go any further than that. So lay low on the idea that you want a child yesterday.

Marital status was discussed earlier. Again, you must remember why you are using a dating service. If it's just to have a physical relationship, make sure that's exactly what he wants to. If you want a long-term relationship make sure he is available for a long-term relationship. If you're still married, just say so, then we can decide whether to delete or try to find out more "specific" details. (As most of you people have found, "married" is not one of the options that you can choose in this category. Gee Goober, I wonder why. You'll have to include it in the narrative. Right!) If you're separated, put separated, don't put that you are divorced. These words have different meanings in case you haven't figured it out by now. Please help us out. Dating is difficult enough, let alone having to waltz around these obviously complicated issues.

In reference to ethnicity, I've seen where people will limit this to one—maybe two ethnic backgrounds, or they will just put "Any." This can be a touchy category. You don't want to sound prejudicial but you don't want to waste people's time either. I have seen some very specific requests like "Only Seeking Big, Black, Beautiful Women," and "Seeking Asian Women Only." One guy was even more specific than that; he said he wanted a "blonde" Asian. Jeepers, that's like looking for a tall midget. Good luck with that one, pal.

Don't worry about what others will think; this is why they have options for us to choose from. Everyone is different and everyone likes different things.

The age category just tickles me to death. I know it's tough putting a lower limit and an upper limit on age, but it can play a significant role. There are some with a very narrow age bracket and others who put "Any." I highly recommend not going below eighteen and personally I'd keep it under 100.

Well, one thing's for sure. A woman's age is no longer a big fat secret like it was years ago. Before Internet dating, men were looking for a slap on the face if they asked a woman her age. Now he doesn't have to. We've already done the dirty work. Or at least we put an age that we thought we looked, or acted. And now we need to put an age range for the person of our dreams.

I did happen to notice that most guys didn't appear to be *too* concerned about age. If they were, they wouldn't have listed such a big range. His age is 30, his match range is 23-27. His age is 40, his match range is 20-29. His age is 50, his match range is 18-20. His age is 65, so his IQ must be 20. I'll bet the entire female population over the age of 30 have noticed guys seem to want women half their age. Not ALL mind you, just a high percentage. So if you guys put an age the same or even older than your own, pat yourself on the back because I recognize and applaud you.

What do I dare say about this age thing? It's been long standing that guys, especially those who fall into this "middle age" range, feel they *need* to be with a younger woman to make them *feel* younger. If I were a guy dating someone half my age, the only thing I would *feel* is like I was a babysitter.

Every once in a while you will see a younger man with an older woman, but not very often. It's like there's an ancient, secret law dating back to cave man days that the man is required to be older. If this is indeed the case, I certainly haven't seen any bills in Legislation that will be changing this anytime soon. However, thanks to the many female schoolteachers out there who are dating their twelve-year-old students, they could be passing a new bill to make this okay any minute now.

Now honestly guys, do you think you can find your soul mate in a gal half your age? I can only imagine how fun your first few dates will be. Should you go to McDonald's or ChuckE Cheese's? Do you go cruising up and down Main Street or stay home and watch reruns of *90210*? I'll bet you can't wait to show all your buddies down at the bowling alley the pictures that were taken at the "Senior Prom," I'm sure that'll make them jealous. One thing's for sure, you could definitely be an influence in helping your date with her homework, especially with their history lesson, since you were there! Am I being harsh? You bet. But someone had to say it; heaven knows we gals all think it.

Guys, would it be so terrible to go out with someone a little closer to your age? Today's forty-year-old is way younger than the 1950's forty-year-old. There's so much more we can do today to help us stay young. Hair dye, contacts, better education on health and fitness, and for gosh sakes, plastic surgery. God would not have put plastic surgeons on this earth if He didn't feel a need to apologize for saddling us with gravity. Plus, if you're out with a woman closer to your age you won't have to keep telling people, "No, this *isn't* my daughter, it's my girlfriend."

Glancing through the women's ads I'd assume they would naturally put an age range at least ten years older, you know, so they could be on a more equal intellectual level. Oh, hold on to your trousers, guys, I was just kidding...kind of. A good percentage of women put an age range between five years younger to ten years older. Again, this is a personal preference; you will be the only one that can answer this question to your liking.

If you're forty-eight and you respond to a person's ad who is 20-30, don't be too disappointed if you don't hear back from them. You may think you would be perfect for them, but maybe you're a little older than what they're looking for. If you go outside the parameters set in someone's ad, there is a chance the person could respond, but be prepared for rejection if they don't. Think twice before you set yourself up for a letdown. Be realistic, people.

Now that you know what your perfect date is going to look like, how far are you willing to travel to meet them? (You already know my personal driving limits.) The answer could depend on where you live. If you live in a small town of 600 in the middle of Nebraska, you may want to extend your distance a tad to increase the chances of finding someone who is available. If you live in a small city in Kentucky, you may want to extend the mileage scale to increase your chances of not finding someone who is "kinfolk."

But if you live in a large metropolitan area, a ten-mile radius could give you ample opportunity to meet your lovey dove. You just need to decide what will best fit you and your lifestyle. Another thing to think about is that no matter where you live, busy schedules may be one reason to seek out people in a tighter mileage zone. There's nothing like putting in a ten-hour day then driving 100 miles to meet someone for a drink.

Laziness could be another reason for listing a small driving radius. One guy wrote in his narrative that he was a homebody, and sure enough when I looked at how far he was willing to travel to meet the love of his life, he put down within *five* miles of his home. Alrightythen. To me, that's really limiting fine quality choices, unless you live in a place like Tokyo. Five miles, wow. All I can say is for all you little old ladies, children, and four-legged creatures, beware!

Or if you run across an ad where the guy lists that he is not willing to travel any farther than from the couch to the TV to see anyone, I personally would delete him. But if he looks like a keeper, you can always hide the remote!

Men tell me they receive emails from all over the world. Yes, you do have the ones who don't mind and some that actually prefer women who are "far away." But for the most part, guys are looking for someone within "touching" distance. Even if the guy specifies they want someone within twenty-five miles, women from all over the globe will still respond, believing that they will be the one who will sway the guy into wanting a long distance relationship. Again, go ahead and respond. Just don't be too discouraged if the guy's not willing to travel half way around the world to meet you. Some women get it in their head that just because they're attractive, the guy will "go the distance" for them, and unfortunately, it is usually just a waste of the guy's time and frustrates the hell out of them. Delete and move on.

The above categories are all pretty important; I mean the dating services wouldn't include them on the profile if they weren't. So for all of you picky people, now's the time to put down exactly what you want. Speak now, or forever hold your peace.

I do have to wonder, by having so many categories, are we becoming so "detail-oriented" that the list we're compiling is going to be next to impossible to fill? Are we being too demanding? Where do we draw the line? What if the guy wants someone between the ages of 34 and 43 and we're 44, do we answer? What happens if you're compatible in most categories, but you have an average build and they're looking for an athletic build? Do we bypass it or take our chances of getting rejected based on one strike? Would they prefer an athletic 45-year-old verses a 35-year-old "thick" person? Are people willing to bend in these categories, or are they etched in stone? I do believe I feel a Tylenol moment coming on.

I'm sure people spend quite a bit of time trying to figure out what to put down. The funny thing is, it doesn't really matter. Here's what I've discovered: you could put down very specific requirements and people who don't fit *any* of them will still answer. One can spend hours trying to figure out what to put for their match and when it's all said and done, people are going to respond regardless. Which in a way could be a good thing. Just because you may not fit into one category shouldn't be a reason not to respond. Depending on the significance of the category, it may make a difference as to whether you will receive a response back or not.

As I mentioned earlier, I was fairly specific on a few issues. When I posted my ad, I put down that I would travel up to twenty-five miles. But I had guys responding from all over the country. No, I'm not bragging, well, maybe a little, but it almost defeats the purpose of filling out the profile, doesn't it? I can see a guy responding if he lives 35 miles away, but a guy living on the opposite side of the continent. Get real; have you not seen the price of gasoline lately?

Again, when filling out these sections, they are basically guidelines; we can fudge a little here and there. But the age topic sure can be a little touchy if the person responding doesn't necessarily fall into the age bracket you are seeking. How do you politely tell them that they are too old or too young?

I actually had guys fifteen years younger than the age I posted respond to my ad. Thank you very much for the compliment, but I just can't keep up with you young 'uns anymore. (Although I've been told it's always good to try new things.) It works the same way for the upper end of the range. If you put 45 as your limit and a 67-year-old answers, what do you do, tell him to put on his bifocals and reread your profile? How do you gently tell him you're not looking for a father figure, you already have the real one?

Again, if the age is only off a few years one way or the other, it's not that big of a deal. But what about more serious issues, like children? Yes, I've brought this up ump-teen times, but only because of the great importance it has when finding someone with similar goals. I've received quite a bit of feedback on this incredibly paramount issue; therefore, I feel it's worth reiterating.

Let's say you see a cute guy and you want to respond to his ad, however, he mentions he doesn't want kids. You're thinking, "Hmmm, I'm very attractive, very funny, outgoing and love sports, so I'm sure he won't mind my kids, especially since the twins will be out of diapers any day now."

Are you sure you want to go down this road? The guy stated that he didn't want kids. What part of that didn't you understand? Do you really want to date the guy for six months then bring up the kid issue hoping to persuade him to change his mind because *you* want kids? Would that be fair?

The guys I talk to want what's on their list. If he wrote that he's specifically looking for "Voluptuous South Pacific Capricorns" you better believe I'm not going to waste my precious time answering that ad and trying to persuade him I can be just as good, if not better. Of if a guy in his forties, fifties, or older wants a 20-year-old and I'm very attracted to him, he still goes directly into the recycle bin. Besides, it's pretty obvious (at least to me) that the guy simply wants a decorative arm ornament. Move on, there's plenty more to choose from. Use a little common sense when deciding whether to respond. You may be setting yourself up for rejection even before you meet.

It's tough enough trying to figure out what we want with all the little blanks to fill in to find a good match, but one thing I'm not a big fan of is the Web sites that try to match you up "like" for "like" and "dislike" for "dislike" in every blasted area. They have you list your favorite hobby, your favorite food, your favorite city, your favorite TV show, your favorite tattoo, everything. Then they attempt to match you up with someone with the exact same interests. What are they trying to do here? I'll tell you what...they're attempting to set us up with clones of ourselves. Is that what you really want? They are trying to match you up with...you! Now ask yourself, would you want to spend an entire evening, not to mention your entire life, with another "you!" (Okay, I know there will be a few "yeses" to that, I can't please everyone!)

What's the old saying, "Opposites attract?" I think they're talking about men and women here. I feel it's going to be virtually impossible for these "exact match" systems to work because we normally have a tendency of hooking up with someone quite the opposite. Could you imagine two talkers getting together or two people who both want to be the life of the party? "Love Story" would turn into "War of the Worlds."

Think of your past relationships. Are you neat? Is he sloppy? Are you a spendthrift? Is he a penny pincher? Is he real outgoing? Are you a wallflower? This matching trait for trait is ludicrous. Sure, you want to find someone with similar interests and similar hobbies but you usually find it hard to do. How many women love to dance but their husbands don't. How many men love puffin' on big ol' Cuban cigars and women don't? You need different interests in your lives to build on. Learn about his interests; have him help you with your hobbies. Work with me here.

Most of the above suggestions are simply guidelines, and no one's going to match up perfectly anyhow, so don't spend too many waking hours trying to come up with the perfect match. If you don't seem to be getting many responses, change a few things in your ad, or delete a few arrogant comments and demands and try again.

Most of all, be patient. Give Internet dating a chance, otherwise it's back to meeting people at bus stops, work, bingo halls, and maybe you can still get copies of the latest "Mail Order Brides" catalog.

The "Perfect" B.S.

1. When listing the qualifications you want in your mate, put down what you want, not what you think someone else wants to hear. It'll catch up with you sooner or later if you put down something you don't like to do just to please the other person.

2. When it comes to children, mark what you truly want. For people who may not know, mark the category, "unsure." That leaves things open for negotiation.

3. Don't be afraid to go outside of your set parameters once in a while. Always keep an open mind in this game called Love.

4. Try to be realistic in your "requests." Remember, no one is perfect, so you may not want to waste your time looking for perfection.

5. If you are not getting the response that you would like, try changing your requested age bracket by a couple years, or increase or decrease your height or weight requirements. That will give you a whole new slew of possibilities.

6. Don't let the matchmaker sites "do the thinking for you" with their little, "Oh, sorry, according to our survey you only match this person by 32%." Forget that techno-garbage, use your own good sense.

I can't say this enough, "Think outside the boxes!"

I appreciate the finer things in life,
such as good wine and gourmet food
(Super sized, of course!)

8 Just Sit Right Back and You'll Hear a Tale....

Describing Who You Are and What You Like to Do

Now that you've finally decided what gender you are, what body type you have, whether or not you have kids and a spouse, and what your perfect match will be like, we can now get to the meat of the menu; the narrative section (a.k.a. All About Me). This is where you can start using all the exciting adjectives to describe yourself, and to mention your hobbies, interests, and accomplishments. As with the other parts of an ad, there's good stuff to put in and not-so-good stuff to leave out. Here's a typical narrative that I see quite often from guys:

"I'm looking for someone to fill the void in my heart, to take romantic walks on the beach, to enjoy a special night out at a nice restaurant, and to drink fine wine by a roaring fire. I'm looking for someone who will understand me for who I am. I believe honesty and communication are the key to any successful relationship, and I hate to end a date without a great goodnight hug."

Alrighty. That scenario sounds so romantic and scintillating that it makes my heart melt, along with my mint chocolate chip ice cream. But I'd be willing to bet (Monopoly) money that the pretty picture painted above will probably only last no more than three, maybe four dates. Am I right, ladies?

After a few dates, it's like, "Oh honey, let's just stay in tonight, big game's on this evening. It's just not any game; it's the biggest game of the week. We'll go out later, like after the season is over, I promise."

Hopping off the beaten track once again, I've always wondered why these so-called couch potato sports junkies are even looking to have a woman around. After all, we just fidget and talk during the game, ask stupid questions and nag all night long. But then I realized why they *do* what us around; they need somebody to fetch their chips and beer for them. Note: If you find out your dating prospect is the proud owner of the 850 sports channel satellite package, you may want to reconsider pursuing a relationship. Chances are his availability may be limited, especially during football, basketball, baseball and hockey season, which if you haven't figured out, runs year-round.

I'm also trying to figure out why people take precious time out of their hectic, stressful lives to list the fact that they like dining out, movies and walks on the beach. Of course, we all like that stuff. If we didn't we'd all starve to death and the entertainment industry would be in the red. As far as walks on the beach goes, I grew up where there were no beaches, just massive mud puddles after heavy downpours, but when I moved to a location that does have beaches, have I ever been taken on a moonlit walk along one? Do guys even know how to find the beach? (Surfer-dudes excluded!)

Why is it so hard for guys to mention that they really enjoy eating cereal out of the box, they like to go to sporting events wearing more team color paint on their body than clothes, and that they enjoy smokin' big ol' stogies wearing their favorite blown-out pair of Fruit of the Looms sitting in their comfy, broken-down La-Z-Boy in front of their big screen? We will find this out sooner or later.

Maybe the dinners out and the movie thing sounds more attractive than the above example? Then again (equal time rule) you won't see a woman writing, "I enjoy hosting home decoration parties, I love doing aerobics and yoga, reading romance novels and I especially love spending time with the kids at the Gymboree."

We do want ourselves to sound the best we can, that's how we catch people. You start out doing and saying things just to impress the other person, but as time wears away, so do the compliments, the sharing in activities, and the conversation. Admit it, we all get lazy and complacent. Then we wonder why we're not happy. Think about it.

And of course, everyone is looking for someone to be his or her "soul mate" to enjoy "good conversation and cuddling on the couch together." Puh-leeez. Reading between the lines from the male perspective: "All I want to do is have sex with an attractive, intelligent and sexy woman. Okay, maybe she doesn't have to be all *that* intelligent." And the female perspective: "All I want is a rich, good-looking man to respect me and take good care of me." Oh, like this isn't true and you all know it!! Is there something we can do to change our perspective on this? Can we ever get past these superficial ways of ours to actually be happy with someone for who they really are? Tough questions. Are you willing to take a chance and set aside high and unrealistic expectations?

Am I being too brutal? I'm sorry but a moment of reality just smacked me in the face. Maybe it's not quite that bad, but maybe we can attempt to make an effort to have the excitement last at least through one sports season. In order to do that, it takes energy, which sadly people forget to cultivate at times. Get out of your rut! Turn off the TV and start making some changes!

We all want to say the perfect things, we want to be as desirable as we possibly can via a computer screen, but try to stay away from listing things that really aren't you. Don't tell a guy you love to golf when you don't know the difference between a putter and a sand wedge. (And no, a sand wedge is not something you munch on during a break!)

But do mention that you would be willing to try new things. Tell them you've stayed out of the water ever since Jaws hit the big screen, but if he held your hand as you waded your way into the waves, you would give it another shot. Never tried hang gliding, or water skiing or snow skiing or hiking or camping or fishing? Maybe now's the time to give it a go.

Open yourself up to new interests. Worried about getting your hair messed up taking a drive with the top down? (The top of the car, ladies!) Afraid of breaking a nail rock climbing? Get over it. Guys would rather be with a woman whose hair is windblown and has two chipped fingernails, than to sit home with a perfect statue letting life slide right on by. Hop out of that blasted comfort zone you've been hiding in and start enjoying life instead of pouting about how big your hips look.

Make your narrative as upbeat as possible. No one wants to be around whiny, negative people. And even though you may not think so, your words can sound negative if you don't pay attention. Instead of mentioning things you don't like and things you can't stand, mention the things you do like and the things you do enjoy. Mention that you are eager to try new things and that you love going to the theatre, or that you enjoy listening to hip-hop music, but haven't found the right person to do it with yet. Sound energetic!

What's the best medicine? No, not Valium. Laughter! What makes a dry, boring work meeting more upbeat? Humor! What takes the edge off a tense argument? No, not Valium, humor! Jokes, ha-ha's. Lighten up. Not just in your narrative, but in every aspect of your life.

Okay, less lecture, more info. I got it! The majority of sites are using questionnaires to get people to list their likes and dislikes. At first I didn't care too much for them, but having specific questions to answer can help those who don't know what in the world to write. Some of these questions asked are, "what are your favorite hobbies? What foreign country would you like to visit? What are your favorite foods? What are your favorite pastimes?" And "what do you like to read?"

Having the same taste in books could be the perfect conversation starter. Having a common interest in bird watching could easily turn into a first date. Heaven knows having the same taste in music can make a road trip more tolerable. Ain't nothing more annoying than driving for hours with your "dream date" tapping the steering wheel to country music when you are definitely a rap kind of girl.

Since I don't like revealing too much info until we talk, I usually answered most questions a tad bit sarcastic. (Gee, that's a shock.) I was surprised at the number of responses that I did get, even being sarcastic. Sarcastic, dry, or witty, guys LOVE women who have a sense of humor. We're so much easier to live with when we can laugh at something verses bitch at something. I'm sure I lost a few prospects in the process, but they were probably old fuddy-duddies anyway.

So shine through here people. Put some thought into what you write. Don't worry about putting what you "think" someone wants to hear, put what's in your heart. One wonderful, positive thing you write could make the difference between getting a response and getting deleted. If you start second-guessing yourself you won't come across as being genuine. And God knows we don't need any more "ungenuine" people out there!

One other thing to think about when writing your narrative or answering questions, FOR CRYING OUT LOUD, DON'T USE ALL CAPITAL LETTERS IN YOUR AD! IT COMES ACROSS AS SHOUTING, OR THAT YOU ARE TRYING WAY TOO HARD TO GET A POINT ACROSS. IN OTHER WORDS, IT'S A BIG TURN OFF, SO I *gently* suggest that you please refrain from using capital letters. Well, you may want to start each sentence off with one, otherwise you'll come across looking like the second grade was pretty rough on you.

Try to keep this section short and sweet. We don't want to put anyone to sleep with our lifelong stories. Besides that, leave them curious about certain topics, it may give them reason to write back. If you tell every little detail right off the bat, you won't have anything to bore them with later.

Don't feel obligated to answer each and every question just because the questionnaire is asking them. You don't have to give out more info than you feel comfortable with.

I noticed that most men's narratives were much shorter in length than the average woman's. Gee, now there's a newsflash. Guys are basically looking for someone who is honest, has a good sense of humor, enjoys new adventures and who is spontaneous. Women on the other hand were a little more descriptive in what they wanted. Take this actual ad for example:

"I want to meet an honest, responsible, mature, single gentleman who is caring, affectionate, educated, genuine, interlectual (sic), classy, patient, fun and athletic. He's needs to be a good communicator, trustworthy, able to compromise and is respectful. He's kind, thoughtful, compassionate and will give me the emotional support I need. He will have no alcohol or drug problems, no control issues or fetishes. He should be romantic, spontaneous, a good listener and appreciates nature. (You may want to take a breather here, folks, she's not finished yet!) He will be fun, enthusiastic, enjoys sightseeing, and won't have a problem introducing me to all of his family, friends, ex girlfriends and golf buddies. Of course he must be financially secure and must be able to put a smile on my face. Sax player a plus."

Well she just described the entire male population west of the Mississippi. Yeah, right! What in hell makes her think she could possibly find all this in one guy? Maybe Jesus would fill the bill...but I don't recall that he played the sax. Another victim of romance novels, I can tell. What is up with this? I simply put down that I am looking for someone who is fun to be with, will take me anywhere to eat where you don't super-size your meal, and who can open a jar of pickles for me.

People sure can be bold in their narratives. On the other hand, at least they're being honest, which is what everyone wants, isn't it? Here's what some other women were requesting, (The following are actual ads. I couldn't even make up material like this!)

"I'm looking for a dinner partner and a movie partner. It would be nice if someone would treat me right and respect me. I am open to all sorts of men, but not ones with "back" hair or the "non balding" (yes! verbatim) type. And please know I am very strict on my age requirements. My ideal guy would be a great Latin lover, with black hair and green eyes, with great arms who likes dogs and who is not a convicted felon." Okey dokey.

This one's priceless too.

> "I am looking for a man that will take care of me and make me feel safe. Someone who is handy around the house and that has many talents and interests. I have a great father who has told me what a real man is and I have 'few' expectations."

Few expectations in a real man, huh? That's interesting. Is that a good thing or a bad thing?

Now this woman has a short list but knows exactly what she's looking for.

> "I want a man that is sensitive, aggressive, and even a little cocky. I am looking for a police officer; not for their uniform but the way they hold themselves in life. They are clean cut and for the most part have values and *some* morals. Preferably at least 5'10" with blue eyes."

Honey, I hung around cops for almost fifteen years, are you sure this is what you want your "fantasy" man to be? (Although if you're into leather and handcuffs and stuff...)

Well, I have no choice but to give the guys an "A" for their brief-but-to-the-point narratives. The women, maybe a "C." Now mind you, there are tons of people who have absolutely wonderful ads posted, and I commend you, but we still need more humor here.

Let me see if I can help you out here, ladies. Like I mentioned earlier, there are certain words and phrases that freak guys out. They may be okay to bring up down the road but they definitely don't work if you put them in your ad before he has a chance to glance down your cleavage. The red flag says it all:

Words and phrases you may want to eliminate in your narrative include: "soul mate, commitment, marriage, looking for just a friend, financially secure, spending the rest of your life with, I hate sports, and I don't sleep with guys on the first ten dates."

Even if you don't sleep with guys right away you don't have to announce it to the world. There'll be plenty of time later to make your feelings on this subject clear. And keep in mind, the number of times you use the word "commitment" in your ad is directly proportional to the number of times you will most likely be deleted. (It's okay to put it in the section where it asks for what type of relationship you want, but leave it at that.)

It's suicide, ladies. Harping on this commitment thing is simply dating suicide. Men know that this is the ultimate goal, but put it in first gear for a while. Take things slow, get to know each other and hold off deciding what to name your first child until at least after the second date. The male psyche is fragile; we have to handle men with care. The time to broach this subject is after you've met a guy you're definitely interested in getting to know better.

Other things that crack me up are sayings like, "Seeking Mr. Right." Isn't that understood? Aren't we *all* seeking Mr. Right? Besides a masochist, is anyone intentionally seeking Mr. Wrong? "Seeking a real man." Compared to what, a blow up doll? And "Not into playing games." So you're not into playing games? Don't you know that life *is* a game? (Remember, it's the board game with the little road and cars that you stick blue and pink sticks in to represent your family as you start working your way down the road of Life?)

Anyway, how do you differentiate "games" in life with life itself? Is it like playing hard to get, or not always being available on a Friday night, or saying one thing and doing something else? What? Isn't this just typical human behavior? The definition of "playing games" varies from person to person. So just what exactly is it? If you date someone for two months then he tells you he's not sure he still wants to see you, is he "playing games" with your head? Or has he simply realized, that after spending time with you, that you may not be the right person for him? What about someone who asks you out, then you get stood up? Is this a game? Unfortunately with dating, I sometimes think it's "standard operating procedure." There are definitely no rules here and if you have no rules, you have no game. Did any of this make sense or am I just rambling?

If you're going to play games, try Twister. That's definitely one way of getting closer to each other! Game playing can add a bit of excitement to a relationship, but playing the wrong way, can be hurtful and insulting.

While I have still have your attention ladies, allow me to add a few more comments. I can't count the number of ads I saw where women stated the same things. They mention that they are looking for someone to take care of them, they want to be respected and they want to be treated right. For some reason I didn't see these lines in men's ads. Guys pay very close attention to what you write, so you may want to consider revising a little.

When a guy reads that you are looking for someone to take care of them, they envision you quitting your job so he can support you and your shopping habits till death do you part. I think some women "feel" they have the right to stop working once they get married. I know it is more difficult in today's time where double income families are often a necessity. But it's almost like it's a given that every woman's dream is to get married and then be able to stay at home. AGAIN, not all, so don't you other women jump on me.

Maybe you didn't mean for him to take care of you in the monetary sense and if by chance (a slim chance) this is not the case, then you need to rephrase it more carefully. Maybe you meant to say you want someone to "protect" you, or make you feel safe somehow. You need to make sure this is what you really meant to say. And remember, if it *is* a financial thing, smart guys see right through this, at least the ones who actually do have money.

You say you want to be treated right? Don't we all? Do we have to spell it out? Again, the male translation to this usually is that you are probably "high maintenance," another red flag in the male vocabulary. In a man's eyes it's different to be considerate and kind versus taking you to expensive restaurants, and buying you flowers and gifts every single day. Is this what you mean by being treated right? Again, if not, try rephrasing it.

Try not to sound too "high maintenance" in your ad. This is a major turnoff for most guys. Limit your list of wants and suggest a few things that you can give.

This one gal asked in her ad, "Do you *really* have what it takes?" What, to please you in every sense of the word, to treat you like a queen and lavish you with gifts and be there at your every beck and call? In my experience, that can be very offensive and unappealing to a guy. It comes across like you are expecting way more from this guy than he is willing or should be expected to give at this point in your (non-existent) relationship.

What is it with some of you women where you want so much right from the start, especially financially? Is this an innate trait females have that I am totally unaware of? I hear so many women say they want to marry a man with money. Why? Why do you feel you are entitled to his money? Yes, since caveman days, the guys were the hunters and the providers. Women were raised expecting to be "taken care of." But you *do* remember what century this is, don't you? We've got to keep up with the times, and we need to start carrying our own weight and quit expecting so damn much.

If money is your end objective, you may want to wait until after you meet to express that to the guy. If you write "in between the lines" to suggest a hint of wanting his bucks, guys will figure it out one way or the other that that is your ultimate goal.

I am not "female" bashing here. I am simply reciting statements guys have made to me over the past twenty years. When comments are constantly made over and over, there must be some validity to it, so we need to start making a few changes.

Another area to watch out for is the amount you write about your kids. I see quite a few ads, even guys' ads, where they feel a need to belabor how their kids are their world and will always be first in their life. This is fine and, to a certain extent, understood. Most rational people would naturally assume this would be the case. But the way it's worded, I feel like I would be the one taking a permanent back seat to the kids, if not a position all the way in the back of the trunk!

Kids are a major issue when dating. We know you won't be as flexible and spontaneous when kids are involved, but that's not the issue. When someone writes, "My kids come first in my life," I feel like I'm automatically placed second on your list in *every* category. I'm not saying I should be placed *above* your kids, but at least make me feel like I am on a close level, especially if the relationship were to progress into something more long-term.

One gentleman who responded to my ad definitely let me know he had a daughter and just how important she is. Great, he should, otherwise I would be surprised when I went to his home and saw this miniature female hanging around. It wasn't the fact his daughter was number one in his life, but it concerned me that he had her in every photo he posted and he signed every email with his name and hers. Is this normal, Dr. Freud?

Should I take this to mean we won't ever have any time by ourselves? Will his daughter be joining us every time we dine out and every time we go to the movies or to the nightclubs? What if things progress into an exclusive, long-term arrangement and an eventual proposal, will the three of us be going to Disneyland on our honeymoon?

I'm not telling you to exclude your children in your new relationships; I'm trying to help you realize that if it frightened me away, it may frighten others away as well. A lot of people don't mind if you have kids, but don't overwhelm us to the point where we become resentful. Chill out a little.

When referring to your children anywhere in the ad, you don't need to build them up so much that it will be a turn off to your potential date. You can overdo it with the, "They are my life, nothing will ever take their place, the only love in my heart is for that of my children." This may make it sound like you have no more love to give anyone else. So be careful here.

One thing I noticed that was missing in the ladies' narratives was what they could give or share with someone. We write what we *want*, which is fine, but I saw very little of what we could *give* in a relationship. We do have a tendency of making sure we have *our* needs met, but what a turn on when you can offer something to the guy.

Mention that you are a terrific listener, that you give great back rubs, and that you enjoy buying little gifts for no special occasion. If you don't do any of the above, maybe now's a good time to start. You don't need to tell him you'll cook for him; he'll expect it every night. That is unless you do what I did. I fixed my guy Hamburger Helper on the second date. Guys expect very little from that point on.

It's a great feeling to do something for someone else and not expect anything back. Let him know you are a giving, caring person.

Nothing is etched in stone here. This is a very subjective area, but it is the bulk of your ad. Be creative and for goodness sake don't forget humor. I can't tell you how many people say they are looking for someone with a sense of humor. Especially the guys! They don't want a nagging, bitchy, whiny woman; they want someone who will make them laugh, and enhance their life, and not to mention, cook and clean for them!

So remember, when in doubt, remember the acronym, K.I.S.S. Keep it simple, silly!

Short, sweet, and to the point B.S.

1. List your hobbies, interests, and what you like to do to see if there is common ground somewhere.
2. Try not to sound too desperate in your pleas of finding a mate.
3. Be short and sweet. Don't give away too much information. Make them want to respond to your ad for more.
4. Try not to let the narrative be all about "me, me, me." Give a little.
5. Be funny, and be very positive.
6. Remember to stay away from the scary words like "commitment, marriage-minded, biological clock, just friends, and hate sports." Let the relationship get off the ground before you start picking out engagement rings.
7. Don't make yourself out to be a super hero or someone you're not. The more adjectives you use, the more insecure you'll come across.
8. REFRAIN FROM USING ALL CAPS, IT COMES ACROSS LIKE YOU'RE YELLING AND HEAVEN KNOWS WE CAN USE LESS OF THAT!

"Why can't I ever think of anything to say??!!"

9 Got Writer's Block...

What to Say When Responding

Now that the kids are in bed and the boyfriend's out for the night (oh, just kidding) you find yourself browsing through the personals, and eventually, you come across one that piques your interest enough to respond. You sit down at the computer, stare dreamy eyed into the monitor and all of a sudden it hits you. Blamo! Writer's block has set in and you find yourself at a loss for words. Gee ladies, that's something that doesn't happen with us very often now, does it? Now that you've built up the courage to sign up for this thing, that is after browsing six months for free, and you have a "cutie" you want to contact, quit stalling and get to work.

Okay, it's forty-five minutes later and you're still sitting in front of a blank screen. Chances are pretty damn slim of meeting someone if you keep this up much longer. How do you know what to write so you don't come across sounding like a blithering idiot or insecure weenie? I used to have a heck of a time coming up with stuff to tell friends and family let alone a complete stranger, but I figured out I needed to get over this little hang-up; otherwise it would be back to trying to meet people at grocery stores, bars, and AA meetings.

So, what *do* you write? Well, the answer to this question, I found out, is easy. *Not much.* "Not much?" you ask with that puzzled expression. That's right; remember the acronym mentioned in the last chapter? The one invented to keep all of us from going off the deep end, K.I.S.S? (Keep It Simple, Silly.) You'll want to keep your initial response short for a few reasons. One, you don't want to divulge too much information too soon. It's best to keep them in suspense so they will be curious enough to write back for more. And two, you don't want to say too much because you *still* don't know with whom you are corresponding.

So be very general in your initial responses. Talk about your occupation, your interests and hobbies, and what you like to do for fun, and by gosh, talk all you want about the weather. You don't have to get too deep into your life history at this point, just keep it light and airy. No one likes to hear all the details anyway, even though you think it is important to you. It's kind of like when people write five-page Christmas letters describing every little thing that Tommy and Suzy did last summer. (As if most people really care.) Stick with the highlights only!

I've received responses as simple as, "Nice profile, you seem friendly," and I've also received very complicated and drawn out ones. One guy sent a seven-page story about his entire life, taking me through each and every accomplishment he ever achieved, enlightened me on his unique philosophies on life, and went into detail about what he was looking for in a mate. He lost me after the third paragraph. (Who needs Sominex?)

People get easily bored, especially after going through dozens of ads, so keep it simple and sweet. You don't want to lose them right off the bat because this could be your only prospect for the week.

I'm not sure why people have to tell us every blessed thought and feeling they have. Leave those details for your relatives to listen to. Another guy wrote an entire page about his wants and desires, and everything that he was looking for in a person. He was so open and frank that he couldn't wait to mention the fact that he was married *but* was also looking for something "meaningful." He wanted someone who was "honest" and NOT INTO PLAYING GAMES! SO DON'T RESPOND BACK IF YOU ARE NOT SERIOUS ABOUT A RELATIONSHIP. The guy's married and he only wants the people who want a "serious" relationship to respond? Which doctor botched up his frontal lobotomy?

I love the guys who write back after reading my brief profile and feel that we would make the perfect couple. Considering I put very little information in my ad and only make enough cute comments to let them know I have a good sense of humor, I find it amazing how they feel they could be the "perfect" match—especially when I find out they live well outside of my driving range, they are out of my age range, and out of range with everything else!

Then there are the automation freaks. What absolutely cracks me up is when people, (and I'll bet more guys do it than ladies,) send "form letters" to a dozen or more people at one time. Great, mass mailings for a soul mate! What next, a special on engagement rings; buy one, and get the next two at half price?

I know guys do this because I've received the exact same response from the same person weeks apart. How touching. They've sent the same letter to so many women they don't even remember whose ads they've answered. And all this time you think you're the one and only and that he took the time to answer *your* ad and he thinks you are so attractive and have qualities that no other person has and wants to meet you and just you, when in reality thirty some other prospects received the very same letter. Gee, how special. Why doesn't he just throw one big party and then he can have us all over at once to save time. Then later everyone could drive over to the funeral home together to view his dead ass when we're finished with him.

Yep, many guys write one letter, then "cut and paste" it, then send it to every available girl this side of the Rockies. Does this tell me they're a little lazy or just missing a few marbles? One guy wrote and told me how he agreed with a lot of the things I had in my profile when I didn't list one thing he was talking about "in" my profile. And you guys want to know why you have to renew your matchmaker membership year after year. Geesh!

Beware: If you receive a response addressed, "Dear John," and your name's not John, you could bet that the person sending the letter "cut and pasted" all of their responses. Delete and move on.

If you really want to meet someone, sending out identical letters to many people all at once may lessen the chances of meeting that "special" person. If you address each ad personally, you will have a better chance of impressing the right prospects.

Take a few minutes, read ONE ad at a time and respond accordingly. Comment on a topic that was discussed in *his* profile. Mention the fact that you enjoy doing the same thing(s), that is if you do, and by all means, compliment, compliment, compliment. For most of us, except our mass serial writers, there's obviously a reason we responded to a particular ad, we apparently liked something we saw or something that was written. Let him know what attracted you to his ad. People take compliments like candy, and you know the old saying, "Flattery gets you everywhere." (Guys, you won't even need a map to get you "everywhere" here!)

If he had a great photo (we know what the odds of that are) tell him. Mention what a terrific smile he or she has or what deep penetrating eyes they have, or how pretty the Porsche in the background is. Anything, just make sure you sound genuine. If he has a look on his face like he's been constipated for the past month, don't tell him what a beautiful smile he has. But do let him know what attracted you to his ad. Tell him that dark hair and moustaches really turn you on or you love to take rides on big ol' Harleys. Guys love to hear this stuff.

Ladies, if you answered an ad based on a guys' six-figure income, you'll have to come up with something a little catchier than "I read your ad and really like the incredible bulge in your pants. No, not that one, the one in the *back* pocket!" Try real hard, pretty please, to keep the conversation geared toward the other person, and not on you, you, you, at least in the beginning.

I also suggest that you read more into what is being written than just what's on the surface. If a guy writes "Nice set of...." and that's it, is he worth responding to? I would think twice. In a way he's not even asking for further contact.

There's a difference between complimenting people's attributes and being rude and crude. If you think the above statement was a compliment, fine, but I think it says a lot more about where the guy's mind is. Of course men usually do have their minds "there," but you may want to tone it down a bit, especially if you're truly interested. If you're not, go ahead and be rude and crude so you can spend the rest of your life sending out mass mailings and ordering cheap, blow up dolls.

Of course, there are stories about crude guys trying to take advantage of women they meet on the Internet, so this is why is it so important to read between the lines. If the guy comes off sounding like he's too good to be true, watch out, he probably is. And by gosh, be leery of anyone who talks about "rough sex," bondage and other stuff like that, especially in the first email. If this is something you are curious about and want to learn more, take classes for Pete's sake, otherwise you'll be taking the risks right along with the curiosity. Use common sense! If something doesn't feel right or look right or sound right, run. Run, Florence, run!

If "rough sex" or anything closely related is mentioned in emails, put on your tennis shoes and run for the hills. This can lead to nothing but trouble. Listen to your gut feeling!

I would be cautious about anyone who writes about all the hot, steamy intimate sex stuff in the first few emails. If you are looking for a decent, respectful person it's unlikely this will be the one. Even if you're just out for a physical relationship, decent people won't advertise it right up front. I think "dirty talk" in the first few correspondences is a *huge* red flag and I'd suggest writing off anyone who gets into that too quickly. If things move in the right direction, later down the road, by golly jeepers, talk dirty 'til your heart and all other body parts are content. But use your head before you make any of your other parts available.

One night I was writing back to a guy named Don when I realized he was online at the same time, so we started exchanging a few emails. After six or seven emails I suggested we talk on the phone and proceeded to give him my number, which may not have been the brightest thing to do. But believe me it wasn't the first time I *acted* then shifted into "brain gear." He wrote back stating he would prefer to email a little more, which was fine and probably a good idea, at least I thought.

Now remember this is the first contact we have had with each other. But by his ninth email, I couldn't help notice how smoothly he steered the conversation from comedy clubs to asking how is it that I like being "pleasured." He told me whatever it was, he was definitely the "right" man for the job. He also wanted to let me know he would be the best kisser and lover I could ever have. Gee, I guess *I* have something to look forward to. Besides, I can go ahead and cancel my matchmaker memberships, pick out a ring, a house and the names for our first two children; now won't that be nice?

Obviously I knew next to nothing about this guy, he knew the same about me, I haven't even seen a picture of this inconsiderate, disrespectful, brainless moron, and he is going to be the "one" for me. What mental institution did he just escape from?

So when I realized where this was leading, (and it wasn't down the aisle) I immediately ceased any and all contact with this bozo. He continued emailing me for several hours after that, but when he realized I wasn't falling for his you-know-what, he slowly faded into that Internet galaxy far, far away.

Now anyone who continues communicating with a nut case like this can only be asking for trouble. These are things you need to watch out for. You don't start talking about stuff like that to someone you don't know. Big, big warning flag. Pay attention to this, even if you're hornier than a three-balled tomcat, you need to delete this type of person and move on.

Everyone loves receiving compliments and hearing how pretty they are, but when someone starts talking about very intimate, personal details that make you uncomfortable, cease all contact immediately.

The first few emails should be very basic and simple. Once you have established a little email rapport, you need to decide whether to go to the next level, thus, contacting each other via a device Alexander Graham Bell invented back in 1876. Some of us computer geeks forget we can still contact people this way. (Well, I myself am not really a computer geek, but I sure can play a mean round of Free Cell.)

Writing back three or four times should be sufficient to decide if you want to continue communication. Although I know many people like to write back and forth longer to make them feel more comfortable. This is fine. But you can learn quite a bit about someone from just a few emails, so if it feels okay, go ahead and exchange phone numbers at this point. If you're like me and misspell every other word you type, you may prefer the phone option, if for no other reason than to give your dear old spell check a break.

If you find yourself emailing for months at a time, there may be a problem brewing somewhere. Guys have told me repeatedly that there are women who just want to write, write, and write. It's like they don't even want to meet. Some women feel that if they do write for a while, the guy will fall for them, whether the guy is attracted to them or not, before ever meeting them. Nice thought in theory, but we're unfortunately dealing with reality here, folks.

I've also had guys tell me they want to learn "everything" about me before we talk. Can't you find out "everything" about me on the phone or during the expensive meal you're going to buy me? Well excuse me; I have no idea who you are and if you even exist. Until then you will be receiving short, nondescriptive details and that's it. In the meantime, relax and take a chill pill.

A good rule of thumb (why is it always a good rule of "thumb?" Can't it be a good rule of index finger or pinky finger? Never mind.) would be if you haven't exchanged numbers after five or six emails, let the person know where they may be able to find a good "Pen Pal Program," wish them luck with the rest of their lives, and move on to the next eligible "ad."

Email enough times to get a good feeling about the person, then, at some point, take the plunge and request to hear their voice. After several phone conversations, either meet or move on, that is unless distance or scheduling conflicts are factors. Matchmaker sites were designed to make it possible to meet people, not to write or talk forever. If this is your intention, your best bet is to try the 900 number phone service. There you can talk until you max out every credit card you own. So if you're not serious about actually *dating*, quit wasting people's time here.

Remember, the object of responding is to get to the point of physical contact—whether it's a cheerful handshake or something more. So take advantage of it—get out of cyberspace and meet *some* place!

Plenty of B.S.

1. Answer each ad personally. Don't use "form" letters to respond. These come across as cold and very impersonal.

2. Tell the person what attracted you to their ad. Let them know you enjoyed reading their profile. And remember, compliment, compliment, compliment!

3. If the other person starts emailing about "rough sex" or anything that's too intimate or personal, delete and move on.

4. Don't go into too much detail right away. You still don't know whom you are talking to, even if they seem like the trustworthiest person since Abe Lincoln.

5. On average, three or four emails should be sufficient before talking on the phone. You don't want to email too long, that indicates that there might be an intimacy problem brewing.

"I wonder how *young* you can be an old maid?"

10 Why Haven't You Called... I Mean Emailed?

When to Respond

Instant gratification. We all want it and we all want it now. (Gee, I wonder if that's why they call it *instant*?) Fast, immediate, ASAP, right away, these words are commonplace in the world in which we live today. We have no patience and we want everything yesterday, or sooner! (Especially when it comes to weekends, paydays, and chocolate cake.)

The explosion of drive thrus back up this theory. There's a drive thru for everything imaginable. These days we don't even have time to sit down to eat let alone chew each bite seventeen times. I even saw where there was a drive thru at a funeral home, you know, for those who have no time to mourn the loss of a loved one who you *most* likely will never see again. What's up with this?

And heaven forbid if we have to wait four seconds for our computer to give us information which used to take us not only hours, but sometimes days to get. Remember when we had to drive to the library, try to figure out the card index, then wander aimlessly around hunting for Dewey Decimal and his "convenient system," looking for the book which should be nestled in the above described section on the topic we need to research only to find out that this particular branch does not have in stock the exact book we just spent hours looking for? (Was that a run on sentence or what?)

I do have to laugh when it comes to my computer. I'm too cheap to pay for the faster Internet service so I patiently wait for my computer to catch up with world events while my clothes slowly go out of style. Mine is so slow that by the time it finishes downloading, all the guys' photos are outdated.

Which brings me, finally, to the point about how anxious and impatient we become waiting for responses from someone we just emailed from the personals. You probably just spent hours going through all the ads, and finally found a few you wanted to respond to. Knowing this is a numbers game; it's best to answer three to six in hopes at least one will think you're cute enough to contact.

Then after we hit the send key, we sit at our desk impatiently waiting for a reply within the next 2.1 nanosecond. And as each second slowly passes by without a response, we slowly become sad, then disappointed, angry, depressed and then suicidal.

"Oh my gosh, he's not going to reply. It was stupid for me to write. What was I thinking? How could I have thought that he would be interested in me? I'll bet it was my hair, I knew I should have worn it down in my picture. And the blouse I had on, it is so old. Maybe heavier makeup or maybe I had too much on. How about colored contacts. More Botox. Waxed! I should have waxed my eyebrows and lip. I'm just going to crawl back under that dumb ol' rock I've been hiding under for the past decade and stay there till Hawaii freezes over."

After waiting six hours without getting a response you finally decide to go to bed. You toss and turn all night, pulling your hair out trying to figure out what's wrong with you. You start blaming yourself, then your parents for all of your faults and shortcomings. But finally the Sandman comes and before you know it, it's morning.

A little suggestion: If a guy doesn't get back to you within two hours of you responding to his ad, tell the firing squad to hold off for a few more hours. Give the guy time to get home from work and unwind.

Years ago you would wake up and have just enough time to get out of bed, jump in the shower, inhale a cup of coffee and head out the door. You never seemed to wake up early enough to sit down for breakfast and read the morning newspaper. You would hit the snooze button more times in one hour than Sammy Sosa would hit home runs in one season. But today you miraculously jump out of bed quicker than you did as a kid on your first day of summer vacation just to check the good ol' personal ads to see if Don Juan or Hotlips Hannah answered your letter.

After checking your email, to your surprise, not one, but five responses are awaiting your arrival. Holy Cow. All of a sudden your homicidal tendencies quickly disappear, male/female bashing comes to a sudden stop and everything's coming up roses for you and for me!

You sit down to go through the responses even before you plug in the coffee maker. What other inconceivable thing could possibly happen? Are cops going to give up jelly-filled donuts? One person after another thanked you for answering their ad. They said your photo was great and wanted to find out more about you. You go through each and every one over and over allowing your self-esteem to soar to heights it's never been before.

You email your friends to let them know that you finally got rid of the cobwebs in your "in box" and that you woke up to a handful of emails. Chances are looking pretty good that you'll most likely have a date for this coming weekend. The excitement makes you lose all track of time and you find yourself high-tailing it off to work with a big grin on your face.

Then, when you arrive two hours late at work your boss not only smiles politely and says hello, but excuses your tardiness due to the fact he arrived only minutes earlier because he was at home doing the exact same thing.

It's so exciting to write someone, and then actually get a response back. But admit it, we have less patience than a dead doctor. People not only check their email daily, they do it on an average of 138 times a day. Which then makes the number of times you check it directly proportional to the depth of the emptiness you feel when there are no new messages each log-on.

It really wouldn't surprise me if the number of office affairs has drastically dropped due to the high volume of email checks, or if restaurants lose business, and gossip at the water coolers is down; no one wants to leave their computers anymore.

It sort of brings me back to the "Stone Age" when we used to give out our phone number and would get so pissed off if we didn't get a call the next day. It's the same thing with the computer. Each hour there's not an email our blood pressure soars up ten points. But when we do get a reply, orgasmic-level fireworks go off alerting everyone in the office of this momentous occasion.

So we keep sneaking on the computer to reread our "personals" responses while slowly becoming guilt-ridden as we try to ignore the pile of paperwork stacked on the desk. Do we file the invoices for the boss first or do we drop a short note back to our potential Friday night date? Our paycheck tells us we better do a little work, and then we can do a little lovin'.

So is there etiquette as to the time frame we should respond? We don't want to appear anxious or desperate, but then again we are, aren't we? After hours of anguish, you decide now is as good a time as ever to respond so you go ahead and write back that evening. But then the process starts all over again waiting for his *second* response. You sit there all day wondering if you said the right thing, or if you said too much, too little, or you start wondering if you're the wrong astrological sign, or maybe he's wanting a blonde, or is he going to have problems with your three adorable kids?

One word: Chill out! (Okay, that was two words, but if you say them real fast, it kind of sounds like one word.) You don't have to spend every breathing moment fixated on the computer. Take a deep breath, do some chores, exercise or catch up on the local news. Or try something different like playing with the kids or calling Grandma and Grandpa. Believe it or not, your computer will still be there when you return. Plus, if people start commenting on the fact that you are starting to resemble your computer, it could be that you're spending way too much time in front of it. Back off a little.

Realistically, "some" time should go by before responding, at least to the initial response. If you respond the minute you receive it, it gives the recipient the idea that you're online twenty-four hours a day, thus giving him the idea you have no life, even though this may be the truth. I read once "you should wait at least twenty-four hours before responding" so that your desperation doesn't pour through. That's twenty-four hours after *each* and *every* email. One a day? Boy, someone out there sure has a lot of time on her hands. One day for the first response is fine, but not after every single correspondence. Now if you're twenty-five years old and have all the time in the world, fine, wait to write back until your little heart's content. But there are some people out there who are so old they don't even buy green bananas. Respond *whenever*, just don't get all stressed out over it. Besides, the other person is probably sitting on the other end patiently waiting for your response as well.

I also have heard it said that you shouldn't write back to anyone over the weekend, that you want to give the person the impression that you are busy. Well I've got news for you, sister; menopause doesn't wait for weekends, and therefore, neither do I! Period. If we were inundated with dates and other activities we wouldn't be Internet dating now, would we?

I used to think women were the only creatures who had absolutely no patience when it came to waiting for a response, but I found guys would email back within hours if not minutes wanting to hook up after the initial contact. They would even want to get together the next day. As for me, even though I tend to respond fairly promptly, there have been times when it would be days before I returned his email because of a busy work project or if I left town for the weekend.

The guy would write back thinking I had met some other hunk and was probably on my honeymoon if I didn't respond the same day. I kid you not. I almost feel obligated to write back within the minute so I won't get yelled at.

Okay, if you write too soon, you're desperate—and if you wait too long you're apparently not all "that" interested. So what's the answer? My advice is, *respond whenever the hell you want!*

Many people will assume if the person doesn't respond within twenty-four hours he/she must not be interested. But I give a person a week before I write them off. They could be on vacation, have a deadline for a project, or are trying to get the soon-to-be-ex out of the house—anything. Or maybe it's because they're wading through tons of responses like I had (yeah, right!) and haven't had a chance to get back to each and every one.

Don't let the length of time between responses set the course for the outcome of a possible meeting. If the person doesn't respond by the next day, don't write them off, and don't take it personally. Just because you check your email 138 times a day doesn't necessarily mean that everyone else does, too!

Here's a question I get asked a lot: "If I don't hear back from someone I am very interested in, should I contact him/her again?" The answer is, certainly! If you're really interested in the person, absolutely try again. There's a small chance they could have deleted your letter by mistake or just didn't have time to reply. If you don't hear from them after a second time, I would back off and let them make the next move. If after two correspondences you don't hear a word, it's a safe bet that he/she moved on to bigger and better emails.

I've been surprised more than once by the question, "Should I send a letter 'telling off' someone who never wrote back?" Yeah, if you're a lowlife and have the scruples of a skunk. There is no law stating anyone *owes* you a response, so why do you feel you have to let him or her know you are a total idiot by blowing your top at someone you don't even know. Yes, we all hate rejection but what good does it do to send nasty letters? Does it make you a "bigger" person for doing it? Are you proud that you got the last word in? Great, carry on. Do you think you'll ever get a date with an attitude like that? I don't think so, Tim.

Don't waste your energy, time, and whatever else to write a "hate" letter to someone simply because they didn't respond to your ad or didn't call when they said they would. Chill out.

All an angry letter is going to do is temporarily elevate your stress level. Let it go. Don't sit and try to figure out why they didn't write back. Also, they may find themselves one day wondering if they blew it by not giving you a chance. But if you send them a scathing missive, they'll have proof positive they made the right choice in *not* choosing *you*. Move on and save your aspirin and antidepressants for more serious issues.

Speaking of nasty letters, one woman was telling me that she went out with this guy a few times and had a great time. He was really friendly and she took a liking to him. She was very anxious to see him again, that is, after she came back from a weekend outing with her daughter. When she got home she was welcomed with four emails from this guy slamming her and telling her what a liar she was and that *no one* goes away with *just* their daughter for a weekend and that someone else *had* to have been with her and that she was a nasty wicked witch (among other things) and he never wanted to see her again. Okay.

You don't need to know why someone doesn't respond. Obviously if they don't, the bottom line is they are *not interested*. I usually take a "no reply" as an "I decided this is a reason you aren't my type" reply and ask no more questions. When a guy doesn't want to continue email communication or phone communication, (or even after you have met and he doesn't want to see you anymore) many women become obsessed with wanting to know why. They feel they have to have closure, even if he only emailed a few times, called a few times, but haven't even gone out at all!

I'm sure people would like to know if they are required by the "matchmaker agreement law" to respond when people answer your ad. That was a tough one for me initially. I felt since the person took the time to respond to my ad I at least owed him a "thanks for writing" note, even if I wasn't interested. My problem was I didn't know how to tell them I wasn't interested. (Plus, people can get inundated with responses and simply not have enough time to read, let alone, answer all the emails. You know, like the "Rich, Well Endowed Doc" mentioned earlier. Then I thought of all the guys I wrote who never responded to me and decided the heck with it. No response is an unwritten code for "Not interested. Move on, toots."

It would be very polite to let someone know that you are not interested. When I first started Internet dating, I would feel hurt if I answered a guy's ad and he didn't respond at all. A "no thank you" would be better than nothing. It felt like being stood up via the computer. However, as mentioned above, due to numerous replies, lack of time, or whatever, people don't or are unable to do it. I actually lost a night's sleep once when I deleted a bunch of emails without responding. I wondered how many guys felt like they were "blown off." Sorry guys!

One time a guy responded to my ad, using a cut and paste generic response, and used all capital letters on top of it, stating at the end, "PLEASE DO NOT RESPOND IF YOU ARE NOT SERIOUSLY INTERESTED IN MEETING!" Well, I wasn't interested at all, especially after reading his email, because it was quite clear that he was an angry young lad. So I was being "respectful" by not answering his ad. What happens? He sends me a hate letter wanting to know why I didn't respond. I wrote back explaining that I was using his "guidelines" for not responding back and boy, that did not sit well with him at all. He fired off an email using more foul language than I have ever heard in any rap song!

If you have a problem with rejection, and it gets you all hot under the collar, well, you better learn how to control your emotions because the Internet magnifies the number of times rejection will kick you in the ass. Get used to it—that or get a dog.

Internet dating can be just as frustrating, if not more frustrating, than meeting people in person. The turnover time is quicker and more voluminous because of the number of people involved. It can lift you up on cloud nine or it can take you down to the depths of hell. It's all how you handle it. Just ask yourself what would you be doing if you weren't meeting people online? It's a numbers game, and your attitude about it has a lot to do with the outcome.

If you feel overwhelmed, take a break. When you feel like you're ready to give it another whirl, hop back on and try again. This is not a miracle cure for the lonely. Think of each experience as a "new" experience, not necessarily a "good" or "bad" experience. If you had a rotten time, remember, the stories make great conversation at parties!

Patient B.S.

1. When you first start answering ads, answer three to six at one time. This will increase your chances of getting a response. Don't depend on answering just one and getting the response you are hoping for.

2. Don't be disappointed if you answer ads and don't get any responses right away. It's a numbers game and it can take some time. (One sleepless night I responded to ten ads, and the next day when I checked my mailbox, I did not get *one* response. It was depressing, but I just took a break and went shopping.)

3. Internet dating can be very unpredictable. You could be swamped with emails one week and receive very few the next. Remember, patience obtains everything.

4. Responding too quickly can give the recipient the impression that you are an Internet junkie, but waiting too long can give them the impression you are not interested. Twelve to 24 hours is the norm for the first response, then anytime you feel comfortable after first contact has been established.

5. One theory is that you should not answer emails over the weekend, thus giving the notion that you are busy dating. I say why waste a weekend alone playing head games when you could be setting the stage to enjoy someone's company. This could also give the impression that you are holding out for the *right* person to spend your weekend with.

6. Sending "hate" letters to those who don't respond to your email only brings out the "ugly" side of you. Keep that hidden in your closet, at least until the next full moon.

7. If you don't hear back from someone after a few emails or even one, don't waste valuable time trying to figure out why they didn't respond. Get over it and get on to someone new!

Tenth Chapter Stretch!
Break time!
Intermission!

I thought this would be a great time if anyone needed a break. Get up. Stretch. Fetch some chips, but don't go too far away. The reason I mention a break at this point is because there is a blank page here and some people freak if they see blank pages and feel they are being cheated out of valuable information. So I just wanted to let you know that no important info has been left out and you can simply resume your normal reading.

...and then at the age of two,
I developed a taste for Popsicles.

11 Blah, Blah, Blah, Blah, Blah

How Much Should You Reveal About Yourself?

It's funny, with traditional dating, (don't you love that, "traditional" dating) on a first date; you normally wouldn't go into a lot of detail about certain aspects of your life. Certain topics are kind of "off limits" until you get to know each other better. In-depth discussions about religion and politics, and especially talk about exes is strictly taboo. But Internet dating has made it a heck of a lot easier for people to brazenly ask anything they want. Not only are other Internet dates discussed, it's usually a conversational icebreaker.

Years ago, first dates could be pretty darn mundane. Conversation usually centered on work, family, sports, and new movie releases. It was almost disrespectful to ask personal questions right away. Now, before you even meet, guys want to know what you do, your age and weight, education, if you want to have kids, your astrological sign, and how many tattoos, scars and body piercings you have.

The topic of "wanting future kids" was definitely something that wasn't mentioned on the first or second date. That signified leading up to some type of commitment. If you asked a guy if he wanted kids during the main course of his meal, you could potentially put him at risk for being a Heimlich maneuver candidate. While he is gagging on that last piece of steak, his life's flashing right before his eyes. He's visualizing his workout room turning into a nursery, giving up his Wednesday night poker game with the boys, and trading his sports car in for a minivan. Before you know it, he's getting up, backing toward the men's room, hoping all the way there that the window will be big enough for him to squeeze through. All the while, his date is sitting there with her mouth wide open wondering what in the buh-jeezes just happened.

Even today, by knowing too much stuff in advance, I think there's a tendency for some good prospects to slip through our fingers sooner than they should. "Oh gee, she drives an SUV and I absolutely cannot date a woman who drives an SUV." But if you were to meet her in person and were attracted to her, and you didn't know what kind of car she drove, it probably wouldn't be an issue when you did find out. That's because you were attracted to her for the qualities you could see, hear, and yes, sometimes feel, when you were together. (By the way, there was a guy that put in his ad that if you drove an SUV, there was no need to reply.) My response to him was if you're that insecure about your masculinity, *you* need not reply. Moron.

But now we don't even get the chance to be cute, charming and funny because we've already been ruled out on a technicality. I believe this could be a fatal pattern that is developing with Internet dating. You rule out someone because they don't eat Sushi or they don't follow major league sports. So what? What does that have to do with the price of French Fries in Paris? I think a lot of good candidates are being overlooked. Some may see it as a "time saving device," you know, not wasting your time with the wrong person, but I see it as being too damn picky for your own good.

So how much *should* we divulge initially? Are we obligated to answer all of their questions before they'll agree to meet us? If we hold nothing back, what will we talk about when we do get together? "Gee Phil, I've told you everything except what color underwear my grandmother wears, we might as well call it a night, whaddayathink?"

When our date asks us about our previous marital status (or current for some of you), do we tell him we've been divorced three times or do we just say, "I'm divorced?" Do you immediately tell him the truth because you feel an obligation to "be honest" or do we save it for our wedding day? Is it really any of their business how many times we've been arrested or the fact that we are on welfare? When would be a good time to let them know we have Herpes or some other medical problems? Personally, until I get past the first few dates, it's simple. It's none of their $%&* business.

One topic that should be kept out of early conversation is your net worth. If you hope to meet someone who wants you for who you are and not for your mansion and millions, definitely wait until you establish more of a relationship, based on personal characteristics.

I went out with a guy, Mike, who told me a story about an Internet date he had. He met this woman for dinner one evening and they seemed to be having a good time. Somewhere in the course of their conversation he mentioned he was having an MRI performed on his back the next day. Immediately, she responded by saying, "You're kidding, I've got an MRI scheduled for tomorrow, too. What a coincidence. See, we have something in common already." Mike assumed she was having her back X-rayed as well, but she immediately corrected him, "Oh no, it's not my back, I'm having my head X-rayed. I had a steel plate put in a few years ago and they have to make sure it hasn't shifted or anything."

So he's sitting there thinking, "Dare I ask this woman, whom I'm sitting across the table from and having dinner with, why she has a steel plate in her head?" Mustering up the courage, he finally asks, "Can I *assume* this is the result of an auto accident?"

"No, no," she smiled nonchalantly, "It's from when I shot myself in the head a while back. I went through a little depression period but things are much better now. Did I mention that things are much better now?" Okay.

Now if this isn't a sure fire way of killing a lovely evening, I'm not quite sure what would be.

At this point Mike's mind is going a mile a minute, trying to figure out what to do. He glances down at her purse to see if it's big enough to carry a handgun. Then, trying not to "upset" her, he tells her he has to go to the men's room. He put money down on the table to pay the bill and told her she may want to go ahead and take off because he wasn't feeling very well, and may be a while. He literally stayed in the restroom half an hour waiting for her to leave so he wouldn't have to confront her. He later admitted to himself that he acted a little irrational, but had panicked and didn't know what else to do.

Do you feel she shared a tad bit more information than she really needed to? If she had half a brain, you'd think she would have waited until at least the third or fourth date to drop this bombshell, don't ya think?

It's amazing it didn't occur to her that by sharing this tidbit this early on might potentially ruin her chances of having a second date with the guy. What was she thinking? Then again, maybe she *did* know what she was thinking. I guess if you ever meet up with someone you aren't overly impressed with and need to figure out a way to get rid of the guy, this scenario would certainly do the trick.

A girlfriend of mine was supposed to meet a guy for a late afternoon drink. They were going to hook up around 4:00 p.m. and just plan the afternoon from there. Now mind you, this is the first time she will be meeting the guy, so I'm sure she dolled herself up and I'm sure the guy wanted to make a good first impression as well. After being with the guy no more than one minute, it was obvious that this guy didn't have to divulge any deep, dark secrets right off the bat; she figured it out all on her own the moment she sat down. She didn't have to "hear" his problems, she simply "smelled" his problem. This guy absolutely reeked of booze, and did nothing but pound down more alcohol in her presence. Either he was extremely nervous about their meeting or he ditched his AA meeting that day. He was probably so confident in himself that he figured she wouldn't notice. Nice try, Einstein.

This story definitely ranks up there with the best of them. I had been communicating with Mark via email and phone for at least a

If your date shows up plastered or even a little tipsy before you even go out on the town, tell him you need to go because you have to watch the final episode of "Survivor" which you forgot to record. Think of anything, just get the heck outta there!

month because we had been unable to meet due to conflicting schedules. (Gee, that's a first.) He "claimed" he was out of the country for three weeks in Great Britain, on business. We had some great talks and one day he mentioned that a woman he knew, actually an ex-girlfriend, had contacted him to ask if he could write a short story for a publication she was working on. I'm not sure why she asked *him* to do this because the guy had told me he was a financial planner. But anyway, she was looking for a story about a couple spending a very romantic afternoon together. After completing his "assignment" he asked me if I would read it and give him my opinion. Sure, I have plenty of time, since we won't be having dinner anytime soon.

He sent the story and for some reason I kept forgetting about it. Every time we talked he asked if I had read it. He seemed extremely anxious for me to give him my feedback. So I finally sat down and read his four-page short story.

Well, I have to admit, his story was one of the most descriptive ones I have read in a while. He used a lot of adjectives I hadn't seen since the last time I browsed through a Hustler magazine. Holy mackerel, I thought! Was he trying to submit work to Larry Flynt here or what? My goodness, I was sitting there with my mouth wide open after reading just the first few lines.

He had written like an XXX-rated story. It was way beyond X-rated, close to a Y or Z-rated story if there is such a thing. What was his objective in sending a story like this to someone he had never met? Was it a hidden message to see how I would react? Was he trying to find out if this would get me all hot and bothered so I would run down and meet him in the middle of the afternoon? Well it did bother me but not in the fashion he would have liked, I am sure. This made no sense to me at all. But instead of trying to figure out his subliminal message, I simply hit the delete key and moved on.

This last one is truly a classic. I couldn't have made up a better story. Charles was the top choice from the guys who answered my first ad. I liked everything about him, and he matched my "qualifications" to a tee, with the exception that he lived three hours away. (You can't have everything.) Like with every other Tom, Dick and Harry, it was weeks before we could get together because he was out of town. In the meantime he would write fairly lengthy emails so I could "get to know him better." I guess he felt that since he was being open and honest that I would be willing to do the same. You know me, I can't blab out every detail about my life too soon to a perfect stranger, no way. Now if it's a stranger I met standing in line to the ladies room, that's a different story.

Digressing a little, it still amazes me how open someone can be through emails versus talking over the phone. With a lot of guys I would have really nice conversations on the phone, but emails always seem to get a tad bit more intimate sooner than I like. I hate it when guys go from talking about what movies they like to asking what do I sleep in, or do I like taking showers with strange, naked men. It totally creeps me out. It just seems out of place to talk about things like this, that is if you're looking for a *decent* person to be with. If not, that's your choice.

The one thing that the Internet does is to allow anonyminity until you're ready to move on to the phone conversation. I think that is why some people feel bolder than others to jump right in and say what they darn well please. Annonyminity allows you to be fun, warm, loving and as playful as you want. I'm sure more than a few of you out there enjoy the "playfulness" over the Internet, but if *I'm* going to be playful, it ain't gonna be online!

Now, back to my story. I really did enjoy our chats, even though he asked more questions than a suspicious police detective. But then out of the clear blue sky he drops the proverbial bombshell. He called the night before we were to meet to let me know he had just emailed some last minute info about himself. Well, he accomplished that task all right.

I found out a smidge more than I really needed to know before our first meeting, which I certainly could have done without. He had written out a list of his likes and dislikes, which we all have, but I have to wonder what his true objective was in sharing these noteworthy tidbits with me.

Okay, let's analyze his list. He starts out by saying he loves hot dogs, he loves burnt toast, he loves to shop, he likes to watch the Lifetime Channel, and he loves soap operas. Then he tells me he hates cigarette smoke, he can't wear socks with holes in them, he washes his car three times a week, he can't go to bed without emptying all the trash cans, he can't wear jeans more than twice without washing them, he can't have grapefruit juice in the morning, and he tops it all off with, get this, "and I really, really, really hate paper napkins." (Three "reallys" folks. Can you guess that he has some "issues"?)

Now I know people who hate liver, and who hate flying and who hate spiders, but paper napkins!!?? Please explain this to me. He also mentioned that while at home he *has* to use a place mat when he eats. Now the guys I know don't even use plates half the time, let alone place mats. Do guys even know what place mats are?

I appreciated his eagerness to tell me *all* about himself, and maybe it's just me, but I saw too many, what's the word...*compulsive* habits, and I kinda thought, was he just a little too in touch with his "feminine side"? These are things you like to find out slowly, if never, but after getting to know someone, chances are these characteristics may not be that bothersome. Even though these may seem like minor "hang-ups," mentioning all this before you meet, in some situations, could shy some people away.

I prefer roll-on deodorant over solid deodorant, and I like frozen corn versus canned corn. I have piles of paper work setting on my desk and yes, sometimes on my dining room table, and I really hate that gunky muck build up in my bathroom sink drain. But I don't feel it's necessary that I share this with you! Don't you agree?

Still, I wasn't about to let these things stop me from meeting him, so we made plans to have lunch the next day, even though I knew BBQ chicken wings were probably out of the question. If things didn't work out, I could always tell him, "I'm sorry, I can't date you. I'm a 'Bounty' kind of woman."

We met at a nice restaurant, not fancy enough for *cloth* napkins, but at least it wasn't fast food. The entire meal my eyes were fixated on his white paper napkin that sat neatly folded up next to his plate. As time went by, he went from the salad to the main course, and then finally on to dessert, never, I repeat, never touching the poor, innocent, unloved little napkin. It lay there like it was paralyzed while mine looked like it had been through three hurricanes, two tornados and a meat grinder. I do have to say he was a neat eater, although I never did see what the tops of his pant legs looked like. If he didn't use a napkin, he had to wipe his hands on something, didn't he?

After our meal, we hugged goodbye, told each other it was nice meeting, and then drifted off into the sunset never having the opportunity to share elegant cloth napkins together.

Reflecting back on this whole thing, it wasn't so much the fact that the guy didn't like paper napkins, but more the fact that he felt he had to tell me. Again, I have hang-ups and things I like and don't like, but I guess I'm not one to burden a person with certain things until I feel the relationship is progressing.

How can someone sound so great on paper, or I should say, on monitor, and then hate paper napkins? I feel like this could have been another Seinfeld episode. I never would have seen this coming. Throughout all of our phone conversations, there were no hints of obsessive behavior. What would possess this guy to tell me about every one of his compulsions? He left no room for me to figure them out on my own. Maybe he has a compulsion about confessing his compulsions?

Needless to say, I wouldn't have let a paper napkin stand in the way of getting to know him better, but after meeting in person, listening to what he had to say, and watching his mannerisms, I thought he might prefer one of my male friends more.

We have this handy dandy "tool" to help us narrow down our search, select the things we like in a person, they fall into this well-defined category, and then we find out later that they hate paper napkins. What's even more frustrating is that I think about him every time I see a little, fragile paper napkin.

If God can put a man on the moon why in the hell doesn't he just put them all there, for crying out loud!!

It's not necessary to spill your guts to everyone you go out with, and you aren't being deceptive if you don't. I used to tell guys right away that I was in jail for four years, and eventually I would get around to telling them it was work related, but it sure was a hoot to see the look on their faces. But when they started going to the men's room and never coming back, I decided to hold off on that subject until I got to know them better.

I love responses where guys tell you how romantic they are, which is fine, but could you leave out the steamy details until we at least talk? It's one thing to tell someone that you enjoy long, wet, passionate kisses and that you love to cuddle, but beyond that, let's let the imagination do its stuff for a while. One guy wrote and actually told me how he loved to interrupt his woman cooking dinner by "doing her" on the kitchen counter. Good way to diet, I guess. But I'm not sure *I* would want to eat what had been on the counter while the early evening festivities began. Are you happy to see me or is that a cucumber in your pocket? Jeepers!

On the other hand, you have some people who feel they don't need to tell you jack squat. One of the guys I dated for a while told me he went out with this woman five or six times before he discovered she'd left out a few "insignificant" details. She finally confessed to the fact that she had a child. I'm sure he would have found out sooner or later. You'd think the child safety seat in her back seat would have been a pretty good indication of something, don't ya think? She also left out a second little secret, her 6'3" boyfriend. Oh, and by the way, he sorta lived with her. *Sorta* lived with her? What, he sleeps on a lounge chair on the patio?

One guy I met told me he spoke with a girl for a few weeks via phone, plus numerous emails, and when they finally met, he couldn't help but notice she only had one arm. How do you start a conversation when you've been completely caught off guard the minute you walk in the door? "Well golly Cindy, it's just a hunch, but I'm guessing that you must be left handed. Off hand, how would you feel if I told you I was a southpaw, too?" Jeepers Wally, talk about feeling a little awkward.

I can't blame her for not putting this in her ad. If she mentioned it right up front, the response rate to her ad would drop significantly. But should she have given him the "heads up" on her unusual physiology? Even that would be a tough thing to do, I mean what would she say, "Oh, by the way when we meet, you may notice I fall short in the 'body parts' category."

I have noticed that on some sites they now have a category for disabilities. I think that makes it much easier to let people know. It's got to be very hard for some to admit up front, but I give them all the credit in the world for doing that. It tells me that they are far bigger people than most.

It's tough to say when a person should reveal their disability. Some don't have a problem mentioning it, and others, I'm sure, are uncomfortable meeting new people. This is a personal decision. Even if you choose not to mention it in the first few emails or phone conversations, I think it should be brought up before the first meeting. Again, people will appreciate the openness instead of being caught off guard.

A woman was telling me about a gentleman she met online. She stated that after a few dates, he was very open with her about the fact that his wife had committed suicide two years previous. What he failed to tell her was that all the gifts he had given her over the course of their very short relationship were actually items that belonged to, or I should say, *used to* belong to his dead wife.

She became suspicious after opening a small purse that had no packing paper inside, or brand name tags attached. She also had received several pieces of jewelry as well, but quickly came to the conclusion they were not new either. At least he was honest when she finally asked if the items had belonged to his deceased wife. (I say this guy wins the Chutzpah Award.) He tried to make her feel better by saying, "But I promise, they've never been worn before." The guy felt he was simply trying to impress someone he cared about. So what if he saved a few bucks in the process? And his wife killed herself because…

I tell guys very little about myself on the first date or the second date, usually because the place is about ready to close by the time he gets around to asking about me. But until I feel comfortable I keep my mouth shut. Some people feel that if they share all of their intimate details with someone it can bring you closer together. Okay, sometimes this is true, but to be safe, wait until later. Nothing like spilling your guts to a perfect stranger then never hearing back from him. Then you start to wonder if you scared him off by telling him more than you should have.

Don't feel obligated to share personal information too soon. You may never see the person again, then you may start to wonder if you did, in fact, divulge too much too soon.

Hold off telling your date that you just recovered from a case of syphilis, and that you can't get together tomorrow because you have to visit your father who is in jail for killing your stepmother, and that you need to get to bed early being five months pregnant and all with a child you don't know who the father is. I'm sure if he understands he won't mind. (Yeah, and Freddie Krueger won "Boy Scout of the Year Award!")

Until you are confident you really like someone, keep the personal stuff personal, keep things light and airy, and be positive. Like I mentioned earlier, just keep the blouses cut low, the cold beers coming and rest of the job will be icing on the cake.

Major B.S.

1. Don't feel like you have to tell your entire life story in the first fifteen minutes of your date—or your first few emails.
2. Don't feel that just because someone chooses to share intimate stories with you that you have to reciprocate.
3. Try to keep certain topics like herpes, gangrene, four ex-husbands, previous operations, and migraine headaches for later conversation.
4. Talk about vacations that you have taken, or which college you attended or who your favorite movie star is. Talk about your accomplishments or what you would like to accomplish. Keep things light, fun and positive.
5. Keep your correspondence upbeat and fun!

P.S. And if you don't like paper napkins, please, pretty please, don't let me know!

Oh here we go again. Another blank page!

That's okay. I know you don't need another break. It's tough putting this baby down, isn't it? Just keep that momentum going in fifth gear!

"Maybe I should have suggested we meet at *my* favorite hangout instead of his!"

12 "Where Do You Want To Go?" "I Don't Care, You Decide." "No, It's Up To You!"

When and Where to Meet

Are you a little tired of making seemingly endless decisions yet? Well, you better sit down because we still have a ways to go. The tough part is definitely behind us though, but the most awkward part is coming up, actually meeting your online date.

So the weeks, sometimes months for some of y'all, of emails and phone calls have escalated to the point of finally meeting. How exciting! But any first date can be uncomfortable even if you initially met in person, so imagine actually getting to meet the person behind the keyboard and monitor—now that's another story. Will he be as funny as he was in his emails? Will she look like her photo? Will he have good teeth and good hygiene? She was only kidding about the sex change operation...right?

Let's get one thing straight: This is a date; it's NOT just a "meeting," even though it may be casual. You are not looking for a buddy, a work partner, or a counselor. You're looking for someone to have a relationship with, right? So treat the first get-together with the honesty of knowing your intention.

The fun part of getting together is trying to decide where to meet. Should be easy, right? Yeah, about as easy as scaling Mt. Everest with both hands tied behind your back. If I had a dollar for every time someone said, "Oh, it doesn't matter to me, where do you want to go?" I could be lunch buddies with Bill Gates! Or how about, "Oh you decide, it doesn't matter to me." "Well, I can't think of any place, how 'bout you?" Or "Gee, any place you pick is perfectly fine with me." I don't know about you, but if someone doesn't decide quickly, we'll be eating blended peas in the cafeteria at the nursing home!

How about narrowing it down to a couple of places, then flipping a coin for the "final answer?" Maybe deciding the time of day to meet could make things a smidgen easier. Do you want to meet for coffee during the day? How about lunch? An after work cocktail? Dinner? A late evening drink? Decisions, decisions, decisions…

Frankly, it boils down to the fact that it's all about blending your confidence with a little bit of curiosity and romance, sprinkled with a touch of pizzazz.

Personally, I hate meeting for a cup of coffee in the middle of the afternoon. One, I don't drink coffee, and two, it always feels like a business interview. You sit across from each other at this tiny little round table that's usually dirty, and start firing questions back and forth. Except for the noise people make pecking on their computers in the background, there's no music, no dance floor, and absolutely no mood of any kind. Pretty romantic, aye? I don't think I have ever had a "good" first date at 2:00 in the afternoon.

I get the impression that guys like doing a midday coffee thingie because it's cheaper. They won't be out a lot of bucks splurging on a nice lunch or dinner, and won't feel bad if the "meeting" doesn't go well, especially if the girl ends up being a nightmare from hell. (Vice versa, in all cases from here on out!) Besides, if he's not enjoying the company he has the ready-made excuse of having to get back to work. I personally think this is the same thing as walking into the situation with a very negative attitude. You already have an escape plan before you hook up, boy that's really swell. Would you have the same strategy if your best friend was setting you up on a blind date? I doubt it. So why would you do it here?

I referred to this setup earlier as a meeting and I do mean to call it that because I don't see this as a date. However, the guy has to realize that by meeting in the middle of the afternoon his chances of getting laid after finishing his cappuccino are slim to none.

If the atmosphere is like a stuffy business interview, then you will leave feeling like you just met with the head of "Human Resources" instead of with a potential mate.

Speaking of interviews, when you show up on your first date, cross-examining your date is about as cool as walking around with toilet paper stuck to your shoe. What's up with firing question after question after question? Chill out. Pretend you're out with your best friend or your buddy. Crime-a-netly!

Where would you go on a "normal" first date? I think a lunch or evening get-together works nicely. Nothing wrong with a little atmosphere, a little music and most importantly a lot of witnesses just in case he turns out to be a *little different* than you anticipated. The more of a date atmosphere there is, the more it will "feel" like a date.

Choose a centrally located public place. It's just easier, take my word for it. Also choose a place that if you're not feeling comfortable or you plum just want to end the evening, you can leave at anytime, whether it be out the front door, slipping out the back door, or Heaven forbid, sneaking out a bathroom window. (Thus, a hot air balloon ride may not be the wisest choice.)

I shouldn't have to tell anyone NEVER to meet at one or the other's house on the first date. But people still make that mistake. I made that humongous mistake once in the beginning and was extremely fortunate that nothing untoward happened. Chances of anything happening may be slim, especially if you had a good screening process, but you can't be too careful. We're so used to having the guy pick us up at our home that we may have the same tendency of thinking to do it with online dating. It's tough to say no, especially when the guy insists that he will pick you up, but be firm and decline his offer. (Even if you meet someone in person, this advice should still be used.)

Under NO circumstances should you meet at someone's place of residence on the first date, or the second as far as that goes. I don't care how long you have been emailing or talking or whatever, you still don't know who this person is yet.

Believe me, you don't want them knowing where you live right away. This is so important I will say it again. *You don't want them knowing where you live right away.* Do you give your social security number out to anyone who asks, or your driver license number to anyone who calls on the phone—of course you don't. The same rules of security and common sense are true here as well.

If you go out a few times, then realize you don't want to pursue a relationship, you have no idea how they will react. If they don't know where you live, it's a lot harder to stalk you, or to egg your house or car.

People have voiced concerns that if a person doesn't want you to pick them up at their house that they are either married or are trying to hide something. Don't leap to the assumption that that is the case. Now if they don't want you stopping by even though you have been dating for two months, *then* you might have reason to be suspicious.You don't need to be skeptical if someone does *not* invite you back to his or her place after the first few dates. They may not be hiding anything, just trying to play it safe.

Ending up having sex on the first night stands as another reason not to meet at each other's house. Ninety percent of the time if a guy asks you in, he wants something and believe me, it's not going to be sharing a cup of hot cocoa. If you *don't* want to be in this position, pardon the pun, don't let it be an option. But if you truly want to be invited in this early in the discovery process that's your business. There are plenty of books out there advising against sex on the first night, but not in mine, it's not my job to tell you what to do on *your* date. After all, I'm not your mother and I'm not your gut instinct.

Other places to meet, let's see. Bowling alleys are good, bookstores, cafes, putt-putt golf, or outdoor festivals. I've had not one, but two guys want to meet for the first time at the gym. What are they thinking? How can you possibly get to know each other between sets of leg presses and bicep curls? I don't get it; it's hard enough to carry on a conversation at a restaurant with the waitress constantly interrupting you, (except when you need her, like when you want refills or the check) let alone when you're trying to work out. I'll bet these guys just can't wait to see this totally ripped, hard body of mine squeezed into a tight leotard. Anyhoo…I never even *try* to flirt with guys at the gym; I work out, I sweat, and then I leave.

I've heard of people meeting at places of common interest, like rock climbing, horseback riding, and golf. I think these are all great things to do on a first date—unless of course, you don't rock climb, ride horses or play golf.

Come to think of it, I did meet one guy on the golf course for the first outing. When we were getting ready to tee off, I found it interesting that this grown man had "Disney Character" club covers, didn't question it though. And I noticed he never took off his hat, even afterwards at the restaurant. I knew, and he knew, he had no hair under that golf cap, and obviously it bothered him more than me. Get off this bald thing guys! We females really don't mind and if we do, I am sure we will list it quite boldly in our "Match Section."

Both parties need to feel comfortable about where they meet; that's the main thing. If you feel nervous or uneasy, speak up. If the guy wants to take you for a ride in his "I built this from a kit I ordered off the Internet" plane and your gut keeps throwing up little red flags, tell him to go right ahead and that you will be waiting safely for him on the ground right next to the first aid station.

Make sure you feel comfortable about the meeting place. Make sure it's a place that if you start feeling like you want to head out of "Dodge," that you can leave with ease.

I find more often than not that the guys like to suggest where to go. They can usually come up with some good ideas, but so can we. But before you go inviting him to your Pampered Chef party, ladies, make sure you'll both enjoy it.

One evening, I met this new guy, Tony, at a local restaurant and we hit it off pretty well. After a few hours he asked if I wanted to go someplace else. He suggested taking a walk in the woods on the other side of town. Well, what in the world are we waiting for? Let me go to my car, get my hiking boots out of the trunk—no big deal that they don't match my dress—and start walking 'til the cows come home.

Did I hear you correctly, Mr. Bundy? You would like me to join you on a moonlit walk in the woods, at dark, alone, after knowing you for two whole hours? Do I look like I just got off the "School for the Stupid and Naïve" bus? Give me a break.

I am sure this guy was harmless, but puh-leeez, don't even go there, literally. Being a former law enforcement officer, I've heard about cases that no one would ever believe could happen. And all because someone chose to trust another before they got to know them better.

Speaking of stories, there was an incident that happened years ago where a guy met a gal at a bar. They talked for a number of hours and ended up leaving together. He took her to a park, hung out for a while then left her there all alone. The following afternoon her parents had to go down to the county morgue to identify her body.

The amazing thing was, this guy never even had a traffic ticket before. This situation is very atypical, but not unheard of, either. Now, how many of us are going to go on walks in the woods with a complete stranger? Good. Too violent to read about? Better you reading about it here versus people reading about you in the newspaper.

Like any other outing, whether it be a blind date, an Internet date, or meeting a guy at the gym, use the same common sense you would in any situation. Don't be "sweet-talked" into doing something you are uncomfortable with.

It's very easy to be lured into making bad decisions. We all have, and looking back, we thank God nothing did happen. It's easy to become lax and especially when we're out having a good time, we sometimes have a habit of leaving our conscience (and brain) back in the car. You don't have to be paranoid, just be smart.

As a last point, it's not a bad idea to let a friend or relative know who you are meeting, (his code name, his email address, the name he gave) and where you will be meeting.

However, with the lovely technology we now have, it's much easier just to take pictures of him, his car, his license plate and his butt, if you choose, with your handy built-in-camera cell phone you carry around like a spare organ.

Either way, get to know your date as well as you can in the safety of your hard drive. Once you're comfortable that they don't sound like an ax murderer or that character out of the *Fatal Attraction* movie, make arrangements to meet at a public place that's convenient for both of you to get to—*separately.* Make it a place that's at least fun and maybe a little romantic in atmosphere. And remember, be safe, be smart, have fun, and be home by ten. (Oops, I just had a *Mom* moment. Sorry.)

Indecisive B.S.

1. Remember to make this as much of a date atmosphere as possible. Make it fun, not a "business interview."
2. Choose a centrally located, public place for the first date. Pick a place that if you would have to leave, for whatever reason, you will easily be able to.
3. NEVER, EVER meet or pick someone up at his or her residence on the first, or even the second date.
4. Don't be suckered into letting your romantic feelings lead you down the wrong path.
5. Let a friend or a relative know who you will be going out with, and where you plan on meeting.
6. And lastly, don't take forever deciding on a place to meet. Have a couple places in mind before you even make your phone call. This, "I don't care, you choose" routine is so sophomoric.

Good News!

This is the last blank page. Rest assured, your concentration will not be interrupted again.

Signed,
The Blank Page Patrol

"I would dig my way to China...
er Japan...wherever, to be with the
love of my life. Me and my big mouth!"

13 Over Hills, Over Dales, Over Seas and Way Past Wales

Long Distance Relationships

Just how far would you go to meet your future "honey bunch?" Literally, I mean. Distance can be a real concern when you want to start seeing each other more than once a year, if you know what I mean.

In Los Angeles and any other major city, everything is so spread out that people actually do rate you, on being "geographically desirable." Love all over the world has triumphed beyond the confines of freeway off-ramps, subway lines and International check points, so I know it will triumph past the digital barrier of the World Wide Web as well. Count on it.

The ability and the desire to meet someone can depend on many factors; where you live, how populated your town is, how desperate you are becoming, and how fast the hands on your biological clock are spinning.

How far you are willing to go, er…travel, I should say, is definitely a personal choice. When I lived in Ohio, I found myself traveling a little farther than I would have liked simply because I was running out of luck in my neck of the woods. But now that I live in LA, I can walk around the block and meet more potential dates than I could in the entire state of Ohio!

Another influence on how far one might be willing to migrate is conflicting work hours, or just working long hours in itself. Or if you have a job where you spend all day driving, the drudgery of further driving could make your stomach (and gas tank) cringe even more. However, if the guy or girl is super hot, who cares about anything cringing!

I quickly discovered that spontaneity is definitely out of the question if you live more than a few hours away. Wanting to meet at the last minute for a late evening cocktail could turn into an early morning breakfast run if it takes you half the night to get there. Of course, if you make good time and things go *real* well, I guess you can end up doing both!

Now with the Internet connecting us with people worldwide, there will be new challenges for many who have never migrated past their own city limits before.

The first thing you may want to ask yourself is *why* would you want to meet someone who lives out of town, out of state, or even out of the country. You need to ask, "What is my relationship objective?" If you are a busy career person and weekends are the only time you have available, a long distance relationship may be ideal for you. But if you're looking for romance and intimacy seven days a week, you may want to reconsider your options.

Take note that if you do meet someone who lives out of state and things start heating up and you find yourself wanting to spend more time with him or her, then there will be plenty of decisions to make from here on out, mostly financially. You're going to find yourself using more vacation days, you'll be getting to know airline ticket counter clerks and flight attendants on a first name basis, and you'll be paying out the ying yang for babysitters, kennels, house sitters, and whatever else you will need when you plan your little weekend pajama parties.

And who is going to visit whom most of the time? I'm going to take a wild guess and say that women will travel to see the man at least eighty percent of the time, if not more. I constantly hear where women will use *their* time, and *their* money to meet Don Juan, and then when they arrive, they're not only out the bucks to get there, but they're stuck paying for other expenses as well. On top of that, half the time the guy isn't who he portrayed himself to be, he was a terrible host, a rotten time was had by all, and then the girl ends up spending even more money for an earlier flight back. Where's the justice here? Is this not a two-way street?

There should be some understanding that whoever is footing the bill for the airline ticket, subway ticket, or gas, everything else should fall on the recipient's plate, or I should say, wallet. Is this not a good compromise?

Besides all this, I *know* that most, if not all of you women will end up staying at this guy's place the first time you ever meet just to save a buck, am I right?

I have one thought on the matter. BAD IDEA! Do you remember the advice in the last chapter? This could be the worst thing you do. I don't care if you have been emailing for years, and talking for centuries, you don't stay with someone you have never met in person. You have NO idea who this person is. ALWAYS stay somewhere else. Plan on a motel bill being in the budget for this little rendezvous.

If a guy insists that you stay with him because it would be "silly" to waste the extra money for a motel, as difficult as it is, tell him, "thanks anyway, but it's not a problem."

This story is a little off the beaten track, but it shows how what starts out as a simple, pleasant night can turn unexpectedly into kind of an uncomfortable night.

One night, Eric, a guy I had gone out with four or five times, called and invited me over to his apartment for the evening. Since street parking is a figment of our imagination in certain parts of LA, he suggested that I park in the gated underground parking garage of his apartment complex. I thought nothing of it, until later that evening when I started feeling a little ill at ease. I'm not sure why I started feeling this way. Maybe it had something to do with Eric revealing to me that he had spent seven years in prison for dealing drugs years ago. That info might have played a *small* part in my uneasiness, just a guess.

He didn't give me any real cause for alarm, but I just didn't want to be there any longer. When I told him I wasn't able to stay he got a little weird on me. I made light of the situation mainly because I realized that my car was being held hostage by this big, strong, metal gate. If I *wanted* to leave, I couldn't. Long-story-short, he ended up throwing me his garage remote and told me I had to let myself out, and then toss the remote back on his patio. (And that I did, all five pieces!) No problema. In the end, I was able to get out without incident, but it sure made for a very unpleasant experience. See, I told you *I* get in the same situations as anyone else out there. I've just learned to see the red flags *before* I fall into the hole instead of while trying to get *out* of the hole. Like I said, I have made all the mistakes, so you don't have to!

Just make sure you use common sense and never park in a locked parking garage until you at least have your own remote.

Getting back to the long distance thing, if you do get involved with someone who lives out of town, are you going to wonder what your new "snookums" is doing when you're not there? If this isn't a concern, please skip down a few paragraphs, but if you *do* happen to care about what he's up to the other three weekends out of the month, you may want to read on.

Trust has got to be the number one consideration with long distance relationships. There are too many miles and too many people in between that could "get in the way" otherwise.

As sad as this may be, people have a tendency to "cover up" the truth a little. They may give you every reason in the book to believe that you are the *only* one. And in some cases, I'm sure this is true. You just have to figure out the positives and negatives and decide what to do from there. Just because my luck ran short in the long distance realm of things doesn't mean it can't work for you.

Come to think of it, I know for a fact that some long distance relationships do work out, that's because I have been on the wrong side of a long distance relationship more than once. For example, I had been seeing this one guy for several months who lived close by. One day (On Thursday, April 8th at 6:48 p.m. to be exact) he tells me that he is getting back with a girl he had been seeing in his hometown, states away. There were no warnings, no red lights, and no bells going off. Just boom, adios amigo.

I was completely caught off guard. There were no problems between us, so when he dropped this bombshell, I was in shock. It didn't dawn on me he was still seeing her, maybe because he told me months ago that he wasn't.

So believe me, I have proof that they can and *do* work. (Is there a tad bit of bitterness seeping through? Oops.) I'm just letting you know there is more than just love to think about when you become involved with someone not residing in your own zip code.

Now it's a little different if you meet someone on a plane, or at a business seminar, or on vacation from out of town. It's not like you *planned* it from the beginning. If you start liking each other, then you have to deal with it from there. But if you know from the get-go that you are half a world apart, won't it be more of a challenge? Most people say it doesn't bother them, yet your dear friends have to listen to your whining when you two are apart, and that you don't know what he's doing for the weekend, and that you don't know why he hasn't called in three days.

Distance can certainly be a hurdle but it doesn't have to be a retaining wall. If you're comfortable with the many miles and many people and many temptations between you, don't sweat it. However, if you are the type of person who will be constantly wondering what Romeo is doing all the time, you may want to change your dating strategy—that or put one of those tracking devices in his pants to keep better tabs on him.

If you begin seeing someone out of town and you know you want a long-term relationship with this person, will you be willing to pack up the truck and move to wherever "sweet cakes" is living? You need to consider this. On the other hand, if you're looking to move out of the current hellhole you're in now, than for no other reason, I say call the movers pronto. But if you have family, a good job, friends, and roots, you need to think twice and know what you're getting yourself into.

I have heard a lot of success stories where people have moved halfway around the world to be with someone they met over the Internet. There are countless people who have waited a lifetime to meet the right person, and they're not about to let a language barrier or border patrol agents get in their way. So, again, there are definitely those who go for quality over convenience.

There always has been more of a tendency for women to move to be with the guy than the other way around, at least that's what happened in my ex-boyfriend's case. I know for a fact that his "out of state" girlfriend moved to be with him. That's because every time I drove by his house her car was in his driveway. I only did it a few times (a week), it got me absolutely nowhere except sick to my stomach. This is another thing I highly recommend not doing, drive bys, but that's another story in itself! Anyhow, getting back to where I was, it doesn't matter who goes where as long as everyone ends up happy.

What about contacting people from other countries? What, can't you find anyone out of the approximately 270 million people in this country? I can hear you women now, "Oh, but all the guys here are jerks! I have no choice but to look abroad. Plus, those British and Australian accents just drive me crazy." My advice: live in LA, you'll hear all the accents you want.

If someone wants to date an out of "countryer" why not *move* to where it is that the type of person you want lives? If you want an Australian, move to Australia. Don't you think the chances of finding an Aussie there are greater than if you live in China? Does this not make sense to anyone but me? Or are these the type of people who simply hide behind the computer screen, never having any intention of ever meeting? Do they get their thrills and needs met just by conversing through a piece of equipment? If this is the case you are definitely on the right track. Type. Type Doris, type! Type till you have no more space on your hard drive!

Years ago a good friend who lives here in the states started corresponding with a gentleman who lives in England. She somehow fell in love with the idea of marrying an Englishman. They emailed for a fairly lengthy time and of course she did fall "in loooove" with the guy. But later when he stopped writing, she went absolutely nuts. She was completely devastated.

They had never met and she had no means of traveling there, and the guy never invited her to come see him. But she ended up creating a whole dramatic tragedy over losing something she never really had. And the purpose of this relationship was….what?

Another gal told me how she met a guy, Arnold, from Austria in a chat room years ago. They kept in touch for over a year and as fate would have it, fell in love via the Internet. Arnold decided to come to the states for a visit and ended up staying an entire month. The couple had a phenomenal time. She had never felt this strong about anyone in her entire life.

Things went so well during his visit that she had made up her mind to move to Austria to be with the love of her life. But for some reason, Arnold decided it would be better if he moved over here to be with her. Six weeks after their initial meeting in person, they were married, and several months later they were expecting their first child. Is this a fairy tale romance or what? And it happened over the Internet where you probably thought only strange, loony people loomed. Well here you have it, folks, an actual success story.

Uh, wait, I'm not quite finished. You may want to stay tuned.

I was so happy for them that (oops!) I forgot to include the final, most important chapter of this romantic saga. I almost forgot to mention that shortly after their child was born, Arnie high tailed it back to Austria—for good (probably had to get back to "Mrs. Arnie") and left her and this tiny child alone and broken-hearted.

How sad, but is the Internet to blame here? If she had met Arnold at a pub when she was in Austria on vacation and the same scenario took place, who would we be pointing fingers at? Since they were only physically together—physically meaning together in the same place at the same time—for six weeks and really didn't know each other, could that have been a potential cause for things not working out?

Some people are going to read a story like this and say how terrible Internet dating is. Well excuse me, but the computer was only a link to put these two people together, what happened after that had nothing to do with hardware or software, it had to do with human-ware. Bodies with hormones, hearts and emotions that often over-rule logic, sense and reality.

The coolest thing about that entire story is the girl said she would not hesitate to Internet date again. When she is ready to jump back in the saddle, online dating will be her primary means of landing her mate. (That is, as soon as she scrapes her computer off the cement where it landed when she earlier tossed it out of the window.)

It's funny, sometimes when we meet someone who lives out of town, we have fantasies of how wonderful our lives would be if we could just be with our little "stud muffin." One time I met a guy from out of state, thought it would be great to pick up, move and start my life over. I had this vision in my head of how wonderful it would be to begin a new life, find a new job, meet new people, and most of all to be with my dream guy.

So, one day I decided to drive up to Wisconsin without telling Paul, my out-of-state dream guy, and surprise him with my wonderful presence. I had never been to his place so now I will finally get to see just how much greener the grass is on the other side of the state line.

When I arrived, Paul wasn't home yet. That didn't stop me from looking in all of his windows to see how "our" house looked. I'm sure he was still at work since I arrived a little earlier than I anticipated. I also took the opportunity to drive around town to see what my "new life" had in store for me.

Well, speaking of *stores*, I couldn't seem to find any around within fifteen miles of Paul's home. In fact there wasn't *anything* around within fifteen miles. His development was like in the middle of Timbuktu, and it easily *could* have been *Tim-buk-tu* because I only saw *two* people wandering around and I think the one guy's name was *Tim* and the other guy's name was *Buck*.

This place was desolate. What does he do up here? Where do you go for pizza, a movie, or gasoline? As I was walking back from his house to get in my car, I looked around at what could be my new home; it was a nice place and the best part was that it already came with Christmas lights. Gee, April and the Christmas lights are still up. Hmmm, either he likes to plan a head or he's a very lazy son of a gun.

Not knowing when he was going to return, I made a U-turn and drove all the way home that same night. When I finally got a hold of him, instead of being thrilled I had driven all the way there just to surprise him, he told me it was pretty stupid of me to come up without letting him know first. He said he got home late that evening because one of his best friends had died and he was helping the family with the funeral arrangements. Likely excuse! Is that the *best* he could come up with?

Anyway, besides the fact he was pissed that I came up without "warning" him, and I had spent eight hours driving, to me it really wasn't a wasted trip. I needed to get rid of that tank of gas sooner or later anyhow. It sure did burst that dream bubble I had. But if anything, I gave up the idea of moving, I gave up on Paul, Tim and Buck, and I cringed for years whenever I would see Christmas lights on homes in April.

Maybe we all have to do this, maybe we have to go the distance, (gosh, I'm punny) but how many times do we have to be disappointed before we quit doing it? Me. Once. Okay twice, but that's it. If he doesn't live in the distance it takes to finish off a number one combo meal in the car, it ain't worth it to me.

Before you get too heavily involved in a "fantasy" relationship, check out as many of the details as you can. Dreaming of a perfect life can be far from living the perfect life.

One single mom told me that she had been emailing an out of state guy for months; they talked all the time, and eventually exchanged photos. She finally decided it was time to meet this incredible hunk so she bought a ticket, took time off from work, found a babysitter, and flew from Idaho to Texas. She was so excited she could hardly wait, especially since they had already discussed her moving to be with him, even though they had never met. (Wow! True optimists...a rare breed.)

She became more excited each minute as the plane landed and taxied to the gate. She told me the second she saw him at the airport she wanted to jump back on the plane, or jump out of the plane, one of the two. She couldn't believe her eyes. He looked nothing like his photo, was probably sixty pounds heavier than he was in the picture, and had more arms and legs than he had teeth. Now she knew why he never smiled in any of his pictures. (Itsy, bitsy, teeny, weenie, red flag.)

She said she barely made it through one day, let alone trying to survive an entire weekend, so what did she do? She paid seventy-five bucks for an earlier flight and headed straight back to Dodge the very next day. Will she do it again? Maybe. Should she invite the guy to come see her? Maybe. That's up to you folks. All I know is that *my* driving days are over. Well, almost, they will be after this one last story. The ads starts out:

> "Single, white male, 38, 6'1", attractive, entrepreneur, very easy going, enjoys all outdoor activities, dining out, and loves genuine conversation."

Hmmm, this sounds good, and what's even better is that his photo looks just like Matt Damon. Can you imagine going out with a Matt Damon look alike! As usual, I was a little hesitant about answering because he was sooo cute I wasn't sure if he would respond (typical thinking of us wonderfully "secure" women). Well I did write and he did respond. That's a start.

His name was Kent, probably still is. He told me he loved my response and mentioned that I was very funny, cute and genuine. Go figure. He enjoyed the same things and didn't want to waste time talking and emailing. So after a few more phone conversations we set up a day and time to meet.

After Kent had placed his ad, I found out he moved three hours south of town, "conveniently" forgetting to update his profile. Man, that's like a galaxy away. What should I do? You know I can't stand this long distance thing. But, what the hey, after all, he does look like Mr. Damon, and it's not like I have anything else to do. So, let's fill up the old gas tank, grab some munchies and head for the border.

With a distance about half the size of the Milky Way, I would normally suggest meeting halfway, however, the one day I could meet him, he was busy until 8:00 p.m. It would be fairly late if we met halfway, so I told him I would drive all the way down and catch up with him after his meeting. He said that would be great, especially since his assistant had borrowed his BMW and he was without a set of wheels. Ohhh-kay.

By this time we had had several lengthy phone conversations, one actually coming in at 5:00 a.m. (Red flag, ladies) and felt we were getting to know each other. He even invited me to stay over at his place if I felt comfortable. I told him I would have to wait and see. In other words, if he was indeed Mr. Incredible the answer might be yes, but if he was a goober, the answer would be no way in Helsinki.

So as I'm driving down the highway (is this why they call Internet stuff the super information highway—you're always on one?) I couldn't wait to finally meet "Matt," I mean Kent. I arrived early and took a mini tour of the city to kill time. I decided to get a bite to eat, just in case he had already eaten or turned out to be a lowlife cheapskate.

Kent arrived right on time, but Matt didn't. Where was my Matt Damon look a like? I wasn't sure it was him at first, he certainly didn't appear to be 6'1" as he stated, more like 5'8". Okay, no biggie, I realize that men and women's scales differ when it comes to terms of measurement.

Though no Matt Damon, Kent was still a nice-looking man. He had light brown hair, a nice build, had a pleasant, friendly smile and was very well dressed. He seemed upbeat and easy going.

We introduced ourselves, got all the awkwardness out of the way, then set off on a walking tour of the downtown area. I found him easy to talk to and he appeared to be enjoying himself. After walking for quite some time, I thought it was a little odd that he never offered to get something to eat or drink. I shrugged it off and kept walking. Remember folks, "Eat Before You Meet!"

Kent had mentioned earlier that his office was nearby so I asked if I could see where he worked. (Evidence, women, evidence!) We walked a few blocks and stopped at an old building where he occupied a small office. He told me he owned his own travel company and also managed some rental properties. His office was nice but was about the same size as one of Shaquille O'Neil's shoeboxes. I happened to notice four stuffed teddy bears sitting around, but was afraid to ask about their significance.

Since all we had done so far was walk, and with his office being close, and his assistant having his Beamer, I was a tad bit curious as to where he was living. I figured it had to be in walking distance, especially since his only mode of transportation was a pair of loafers.

Hoping he wasn't residing at the local train station, I slowly mustered up the courage to ask the big question, I mean, after all, he did offer his place for the night.

"So, Kent, do you live close by?"

"Well, since I haven't had a chance to look for a permanent place, I have been staying with a good friend...on his boat."

Okay, thinking to myself, now if I decide to take him up on his invitation, which obviously I wouldn't since I didn't even know the guy, (and he wasn't as cute as Matt) would there be room for all of us on his buddy's boat? I don't know, maybe it's a yacht. (Yeah, and I'm Ginger, and Gilligan will be showing up soon.) I wish he could have at least forewarned me; I could have brought my Dramamine and my fishing pole.

"Yeah, I live on his boat, but he left for a few weeks...with his family...on vacation...using his boat."

Now I have never claimed to be a brain surgeon or a rocket scientist, but if his buddy's on vacation and he took his boat—a.k.a Kent's sleeping quarters—just where is Kent sleeping? And where was he expecting me to sleep? On the dingy roped to the side?

"Oh, I'm staying here at my office. I have a small roll up mat that I keep in the closet that you can use and there's a sink in the bathroom where you can freshen up. I have some Baby Wipes here in the office if you need them. You're more than welcome to stay here with me."

My God, I was starting to feel like Cinderella, could all this be true? An opportunity to stay at a five star office, how enticing! How could I turn down this generous offer? And silly me, I was going to get a motel room, you know, with a bed, a shower, and a TV. What *was* I thinking!

Now let me get this straight, I drove three hours, used my car and paid for gas and a motel just to meet a guy who has no sense of height, no car, no appetite, and no place he could call home. What more could he *not* have?

Money. He had no money. After I told him I was ready to find a motel, he tried to convince me it wasn't necessary and that I shouldn't "waste" my money. Heck, I certainly couldn't waste his money, so why not waste my own. I have so far.

We finally found a motel and after I got settled in, he finally popped the question, (not *that* question)

"Hey, would you like to get a bite to eat or something to drink? I am a tad bit parched after that long walk. The only thing is, if you would like to, it has to be your treat because I don't have a dime on me. Any suggestions on where to go?"

Yeah I do, but the temperature may be a little *too* hot for you there, you moron. What else do you want from me? Well, that was a stupid question. Of course, he wanted to know if he could spend the night with me in my motel room.

Does this guy have balls of steel or just a steel plate where his brain used to be? The amazing thing is that I don't think he wanted to stay so we could have a night of wild sex, I think he just wanted a bed, a shower and a TV.

After begging numerous times if he could stay, I finally told him I was exhausted and dying of thirst and starvation, and that I needed to get some rest. I told him I would be very glad to drop him off at his home...office...home office...whatever.

As I left him on the stoop of his office building, I told him I was very sorry that things didn't work out, especially since he had so much to offer.

Am I wrong here? Was I expecting too much? Please help me out here. Just point me in the right direction to the nearest mental institution so I can meet my next potential date.

It's tough enough to find compatible mates. So you don't necessarily have to delete someone because of the distance. If you do find the love of your life, I guess a little inconvenience will be worth it in the end. Actually, one benefit of long distance relationships is that it forces you to take things slow. You don't see each other everyday, you cherish the time you do spend together, and you normally don't rush into anything. What's the old saying, "Absence makes the heart grow fonder." Well, maybe there *is* something to having a little space between us! I think I've actually talked *myself* into widening my own driving distance!

I think the older we get, the more we know what we want. Certain things may not be as important as they were years ago, but being with the right person can mean changing a lot of things in your life. You just need to make sure you have weighed all of your options before making such a huge emotional commitment. But if you pay attention to your gut instinct, I think you will know when it's right.

Inaccessible B.S.

1. If you become involved with someone who lives farther than you normally travel, make sure you budget for extra food, gas, or plane money.
2. Be sure to establish that the person footing the bill for the plane ticket, gas, or motel bill shouldn't have to pay for any extras after you're there.
3. When visiting your sweetie out of state, or city, or wherever, I recommend finding your own accommodations even if you feel like you know the person well enough to add them to your cell phone directory. NEVER STAY AT THEIR PLACE the first visit (or two).
4. When dating someone abroad, besides not forgetting the Kaopectate, don't forget to date longer than six weeks before tying the knot.
5. In calculating the farthest distance your mate should be from you, try one length of a standard "dog" leash for every ounce of insecurity. That is, make sure you can mentally handle the miles between you. (In other words, if you're insecure, a long distance relationship *ain't* for you!)
6. Make sure you know what your relationship objective is before becoming heavily involved with someone out of town.
7. If trust is lacking going into a long distance relationship, you may want to reconsider your options.

P.S. Before visiting someone way off in the Milky Way, make sure their home is safely secured to something…anything, so that it doesn't suddenly drift off in the middle of the night!

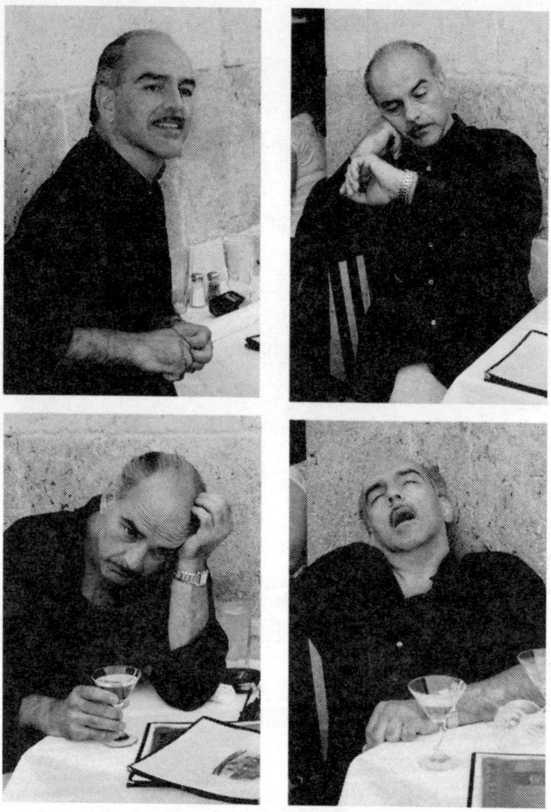

Sometimes pictures speak louder than words.

14 To Be Stood Up, Or Not To Be Stood Up

Never Actually Meeting

Whether you first meet a girl/guy at a party, a bar, at church, at work, or through the Internet, there's a common problem you may potentially face: being stood up. I don't think there is any worse feeling one can experience than waiting by yourself, and waiting, and waiting, and waiting even longer, anxiously awaiting your date's arrival, then…nothing.

Have you ever had plans for a Friday night, spending your typical six hours getting ready, doing the hair thing, the wardrobe thing, washing the car, and whatever else you do, just to be stood up? If you answered no, you either a) have never dated and had a prearranged marriage, b) you are a very rich beautiful super model, c) it is public knowledge that you are easy and put out on the first date, or d) you are flat out lying.

In my opinion, rejection is the number one fear in the world, outranking public speaking, death, and running into Bill Clinton in a cigar store. The greatest need we have is to be accepted and loved, and when we get stood up it's like being kicked in the face… repeatedly.

There was a period of time when I got stood up more often than I would have liked. (Most of the dates that did stand me up were ones that I met in person or through friends.) On a few occasions I wouldn't even finish getting ready, I was so sure they were going to back out. It would be date night and I would sit and watch the clock tick by praying that darn phone didn't ring. (Was I the ultimate pessimist?) And lo and behold, that infamous last minute phone call indeed came through. Did those guys have me on speed dial or what?

Okay, let me get this straight. I just spoke with the guy last night at 10:00 p.m. to confirm our plans for the following evening, but at 5:30 p.m. the next day he calls to let me know that he miraculously made amends with a woman he dated five years ago who he hasn't even heard from in the last four and a half years, and who, by the way, still lives out of state. Gee, Cupid sure comes along at the darndest times!

Oh, and the excuses people can come up with, would make me want to throw up. Yes, both men AND women. We're not off the hook here by any means, ladies. Some of my favorite excuses are, "I just got home and my kid is sick." "I got called out of town on business." "My Grandfather died" (again). "My mother had to have an emergency face lift operation." Or the most over-used excuse, "I'm getting back with my ex-girlfriend." Give me a break, will ya!

This one guy gets an award for "Best Excuse in the World to Cancel a Date." He called and said, "My wife won't let me go out tonight." I do have to admit, that's a pretty legitimate excuse. Pathetic, but legit.

Now with Internet dating, since there are a few more steps in the process of meeting someone, that means there are a few more steps in possibly getting "stood up." The key is how to handle these situations and hopefully prevent them from happening again—or at least minimize their occurrence.

I mentioned earlier that there will be times when you answer someone's ad, or they respond back to yours and you won't get a response, which is something that you will indeed experience with Internet dating. The two reasons I have found for people not responding are that they are not interested, or they have found someone already, and have not yet taken down their ad. A third reason may simply be not having the time to answer all responses received.

I had no idea of the response I would get when I moved from Ohio to California and reposted my ad. Within several weeks, I had hundreds of responses (due mainly to the large number of people in this area, and okay, I wore a tight top.) When the emails first came in, I read each and every one, but it got to the point where I didn't have time to go through them all because of my work schedule, my exercise time, and my quiet time. As I said earlier, I ended up deleting quite a few simply because I had no time to get back. I am sure other people have experienced the same thing. This is a good example of lack of time, thus, being unable to get back to everyone who has responded.

After you continue emailing for a while, you "advance" to the phone phase. How many times have you heard a guy say, "I'll call you tonight when I get home from work?" But the only ones that seem excited about contacting you are all those annoying telemarketing humanoids. It's extremely frustrating and disappointing, more than anything not to get that anticipated call. But for whatever reason, even though not calling wasn't the most polite thing to do, we need to get past it and quit trying to figure out why. Each moment of my life is sacred and I don't want to waste a second trying to figure out why some guy I haven't even met yet, hasn't called. If a guy says he going to call, great, but I am not going to sit home by the phone all night waiting. If you don't expect it, it's not as bad when they don't call. Call me pessimistic or that I have low expectations, but it sure does save on my supply of "worry cells."

Here are a few examples of what has happened to me in the past:

After going through my smorgasbord of "ad" men, I chose Gary to be my next lucky participant in my dating game. I decided to answer his ad because he had a nice photo (I could actually see his face) and he had a super smile and even resembled Jim Carrey a little. He had an informative but simple profile, sounded like he had a great sense of humor and he even spelled all of his words correctly. The only negative thing was he lived outside of my "If I can't eat a combo meal in my car by the time I get there, you're too far away" driving distance. Even so, after weighing the pros and cons, I decided to email him.

Gary and I emailed back and forth about three or four times, you know, within the "legal" requirements for electronic correspondences, and followed up with phone calls. During one of our conversations, Gary told me he was moving in a few weeks within miles of me. Gee, I didn't know I had *that* much influence over him, and we haven't even met. That took care of the geographically undesirable conflict I had in the beginning. Terrific, this is perfect now, I'm happy, my gas-guzzling car is happy, we're all happy.

Scheduling a meeting place and time was the next exciting step on the agenda. Because of his kids' schedule, it was weeks before we could meet. Was I upset about this?

Noooo, I just simply got back with a few other "ad" prospects in the meantime. What? Me sit home waiting for some guy to make up his mind about getting together, no way! But after a few weeks we did manage to set something up for Friday night.

Friday is finally upon us, but before I tell you about the evening, let me describe the real Gary so you can get a visual here. He's, he's…he's...wait, I just can't tell you what he looks like. You know why? Because we NEVER MET! That's right, folks, one month of emailing and talking and emailing and talking, then nothing, nada, zilch. We set up a time and place, then nothing. No reminder call to make sure everything was still on. No email or call to cancel. He just dropped off the face of the earth. It was either that or he got a better offer at the very last minute.

After all the letters and phone calls, I felt I knew this guy well enough to introduce him to the family. I wrote so many emails that I decided to start writing for a living. I thought if I was going to spend this much time writing I might as well get paid for it.

What is up with not calling, totally ignoring a month's worth of correspondence? My first thought was "What did I do wrong?" (Us women, that's automatic for us.) In regards to my emails, did I use the wrong font? Maybe the wrong *size* font. Maybe the font just wasn't big enough or supple enough. Should I have gone for a high gloss, hot juicy red font? What should I have done, Dr. Phil? Please help me out; I'm willing to change, honest!

Practically the same scenario happened with another guy, Bobby. This situation started out the same, emailing, talking then scheduling a meeting. For us, things were going very well in the beginning. He thought I was very attractive, mentioned that he liked what I had to say, said I was very funny and he could "sense" I was a good decent, human being.

I became concerned, though, when after numerous emails he still wasn't interested in talking yet. He said he was fairly new with Internet dating and didn't want to jump into anything too quickly. He also mentioned he wanted to learn as much about me as possible before talking. Like he can't learn enough about me over the phone? Well, I definitely wasn't going to write forever, so I asked if we could exchange numbers. I gave the excuse that I had used up so much of the free space on my hard drive emailing him that I was hoping we could talk instead of me having to download more memory.

Finally after the seventh email he finally felt comfortable enough to talk. Good thing for him, he probably didn't realize he was going to be deleted if he wanted to continue emailing forever. (Again, the number of initial email exchanges depends on everyone's comfort level. I found that if someone drags the emails out over a period of weeks, or even months, it's time to wonder if their intention is really moving toward the direction of actually wanting to meet. People can spend weeks emailing then find after they meet, there is nothing there, and many weeks were wasted "trying to get to know" the wrong person.)

Before we even spoke on the phone, Bobby said he was so impressed with my outlook on life that he definitely wanted to meet. I thought, wow, this guy's got a good head on his shoulders—and has good taste—I might add, and I clearly had a good feeling that things were going in the right direction.

Our first phone conversation was fairly basic. The entire discussion centered on our careers and a mutual interest we both shared, photography. That was it, nothing more. No deep discussions about the future, kids, retirement, exes, nothing heavy, just a casual conversation about work and photography. The conversation ended with us making plans to get together the following evening.

Lo and behold I wake up the next morning to find an email from Bobby saying that he won't be able to make it that evening after all. Gee, what a surprise. It wasn't his canceling that surprised me, but the reason he gave.

He proceeded to tell me what a "reality check" our conversation was for him. He had thought about everything we talked about and came to the realization that he was by no means ready to commit to a relationship. He had done some serious thinking—apparently between 11:00 p.m. Thursday when our phone call ended and 8:00 a.m. Friday when I received his email. He now realized that this was a terrible and complicated time in his life, that he had a lot to work out, and wanted to deal with issues he had been struggling with for years. (What issues? His wife and kids!)

He went on to mention that he was emotionally unavailable and unable to be the friend I deserve. He was so grateful to me for making him see things more clearly. He told me that this had been a "positive" step for him and not to let this bring me down, and not to get discouraged because as great a person that I am I should have no problem finding the love of my life.

What in the #$%@ was that all about? I was totally speechless and completely dumbfounded. Where in the world did all of this come from? Nothing was discussed in emails or phone conversations about anything vital to our philosophy on life, but somehow talking about photography made him see the "big picture." How unbelievable! If Webster hasn't found a poster child for the word "jerk," he has one now.

Why is "Boob-by" even Internet dating if he's not in the "right" place in his life? And if I was so perfect and attractive and everything he wanted in a person, why couldn't he meet and at least say hello? If he had met me in person and wasn't attracted to me for whatever reason, it would make a little more sense. But to come up with a whole scenario of dysfunction before I even had the chance to frighten him off in person just baffles me. I'm guessing his Prozac ran out a little too soon, what do you think?

It's impossible to be able to screen out the "stander uppers" and there is not much you can do to figure out why people are so inconsiderate. But unfortunately, they are, and we just have to say, "Hey, it's their loss. He/she lost out on a great catch" and then you proceed to look for the person who *is* right for you to come along.

The great thing with Internet dating and no-shows is that you can actually have a plan "B," and even a plan "C." One night I had plans to go out with Jerry, but at the last minute he calls and tells me that his kid came down with the Bubonic Plague or something and couldn't make it. Well, I was bummed out for all of about fifteen minutes when Richard, another online prospect called. He apologized for calling at the last minute, but he'd just come up with two tickets to a ballgame and wanted to know if I would like to join him. Gee, let me think about it...okay. Now with traditional dating, how often does something like that happen?

Another night I was thirty minutes away from meeting my date, when I realized he never called to confirm our plans. I had just changed cell phones and figured he had called my old number, which in fact he did, to let me know that he couldn't make it. Was I pissed, or frustrated, or upset? No, not really. What I did, instead of throw myself a pity party, I called another guy, Sean, I had emailed and talked with, but had never met, on a Friday at that! Sean is the hunky, great body guy I wrote about in the photo section.

Every no-show story I hear about starts out the same. If there's enough mutual interest on both sides to continue carrying on communication for weeks and weeks, why is it that these people suddenly decide not to meet? I can go on and on and on about people who email and talk on the phone for decades, but never meet. Why is that? Why are people spending good money to join these matchmaking services, then wasting their time just sitting and typing all day long in the security of their own home, knowing good and well they really don't want to meet face to face? Anti-social? Shy? Behind bars? What?

The few people who are leery of Internet dating have told me that they thought the majority of people on the personal sites are probably socially inept, have little interpersonal skills, are lonely and desperate, or just plain loony. They feel the Internet is used as a safety barrier to hide behind for those who fear physical confrontation. Gee, how perceptive of them. Of course that would mean that *I* must be socially inept, have no interpersonal skills, lonely and desperate, and probably just plain loony because *I* internet date.

I initially thought people used matchmaking services to meet someone with whom they could potentially build a friendship, possibly leading to something long-term. Silly me, I always have been a little on the naïve side. (When I was younger, I also thought the earth was flat, at least in my neighborhood). But the more time I spent online, and the more educated I became, I realized that this was only a small part of the much larger picture.

So what *are* people looking for from these ads? Are they looking for a friend, a long-term partner, a lover or a pen pal? Are they looking for someone to fill a void because they are lonely and are trying to get over someone? Or are they looking to find someone to make them feel good about themselves, or maybe it's to boost their little egos?

There are probably a lot of people that may not know what they're looking for. I'm sure the majority of people are looking for *any* type of relationship. Some people may currently be in loveless relationships, but for whatever reason can't—or won't—end it, and are looking to see what's out there. I know others probably go online just to be in contact with the outside world, even if it's only through emails.

Try to figure out what it is that you are looking for before you waste everyone else's time. If you simply want to chat, there are a million chat rooms you can go to.

There is a sense of feeling good when someone notices your photo or tells you how funny, attractive, and down to earth you are. Maybe that's all we're looking for, a confidence boost. But it needs to be more than that. Otherwise you may have to look for another resource that will help boost your level of confidence.

I know there are tons of people who truly do want to find a long-term relationship; unfortunately they have to "kiss a lot of frogs" (as the old saying goes), who have no clue as to what they want in life. However, until you figure out whether you're looking for just friendships, wanting only a physical/intimate thing, or are seeking a long-term commitment, you're going to have to step away from the buffet and choose your one favorite dish, because right now the only thing you're accomplishing is holding up the line for the rest of us!

Your job is to know what you want, and to have the patience and intelligence to discover what the people you respond to want.

It's funny, some sites even throw in Pen Pals as a choice in the "What are you looking for" category. But I personally feel this should be an entirely separate Web site. Having a pen pal in high school was fun, however, I thought that program was set up more as a learning experience. You know, writing a student in a foreign country to learn about their culture, not to find a potential lover and mate. I have absolutely no problem with people wanting to communicate to anyone anywhere but do you have to do it on a *matchmaker* site? I would like to say, quit clogging up the mailboxes of people who truly want to meet and go find your own site or chat room to "pal" around in!

A friend of mine was sharing some of his experiences with Internet dating one evening and went on to say what a difficult time he had getting ladies to meet face to face. He told me it's like you answer a woman's ad, correspond with her, tell her you are interested in her enough to meet, then never hear from her again.

His theory is that a lot of women are online just looking for attention, similar to the same way they would tease or play with a guy in a bar, not wanting to take it any further. They hit on a guy, flirt with him, get him to buy her a couple of drinks, and boom, she's out the door, if not over in the corner seeking out fall guy number two.

My friend feels some women are basically seeking approval and once they have it, by having their ad answered and being told how wonderful they are, you've just satisfied their need to be sought out. It makes them feel good and they like the attention, even though they stay barricaded behind a computer screen.

If I signed up on a bowling league, what would be my objective in joining? To bowl, right? If I signed up to take a basket-weaving course, wouldn't my objective be to make baskets? Well, if people sign up for a matchmaker site, don't you think the idea behind it would be to get "matched" up with somebody? If you don't have any intention of meeting someone for any type of relationship where it involves human contact, get the hell out of Dodge and don't include us in your host of insecurities and phobias. (And if you do have a host of insecurities and phobias, there are so many resources to help overcome this. Seriously!)

Maybe there should be an incentive program. How about offering free gifts at the "closing." Okay John, if you meet Susie within 72 hours you will win a free ratchet set and a lovely set of beer mugs. If you meet her within 48 hours you will win season tickets to the Cincinnati Bengels home football games. Oops, never mind, the way they've been playing, that will only scare some guys away. How about a free gas grill with a lifetime supply of charcoal...er propane instead? Or, say you meet within 24 hours of the initial email you will win a free lap dance performed to any Barry Manilow song of your choice. And if you call now, we will throw in two free Barry Manilow CDs, but you must act now, offer expires at midnight. Offer not valid in New Jersey.

So you think this is ridiculous, huh? There are probably lots of people who could win awards for having the most patience, but jeepers, facelifts can only last so long. Come on people, get with it. Do you *really* want to go back to blind dates, grocery stores and office romances?

Now I realize that a lot of men out there may have a little commitment phobia, but allow me to let you in on a little secret: You won't have to worry about any commitment factor if you don't ever meet. But you won't ever get laid either, so think about that, Romeo!

What about the women who don't ever want to meet? Why don't you consider taking classes on assertiveness or building your self-esteem and confidence? Go to Jenny Craig, sign up for some yoga classes or take up a sport, anything to help rid yourself of your insecurities. If that's not the reason you won't meet in person, what is? Or maybe it's the fact you lied about your appearance or posted a picture of your Brittany Spears look-alike cousin instead. Whatever the reason, fix it, and then move on, so you can be happy with yourself and your new beau. Life's too short to spend on virtual relationships that never turn real.

If you're afraid to meet face to face, I'm afraid you're going to miss out on a lot of good things life has to offer. Seek advice or help in areas that you feel may be holding you back. Put your insecurities aside and start living.

If you've been doing Internet dating for a while, I'm sure you're like me and have had a few no shows, and a "one timer" or two. We've all gone out with a guy once and never heard back from him again. I don't know what it is, at least with me, I take showers, use deodorant, I smile, I laugh at his jokes, I order the cheapest item on the menu AND I offer to chip in. (Women, if you want to score like a thousand bonus points, at *least* offer to slap a few bucks down for the tip, it will impress the pants off them.) So if we fit the bill, why aren't we getting any callbacks?

It makes me wonder, if we can't even hook up more than once, how would our dating relationship have been? A date once every three weeks, gee, that's swell Wally, but even a woman can get horny waiting *that* long. I realize our schedules can get a little crazy at times, and we can't get together every other night, but if you are interested in dating *make* the time, otherwise it will never happen. And if you wait until the *perfect* time to fall in love, good luck, because there is no *perfect* time, there is no *perfect* place and there is no *perfect* mate. So, you have to make it happen. If you don't want to die a little old lonely senior citizen, get off your tush and start making some hearts throb.

Even with all the negatives that can be thrown our way, look out for all the good ones. Life can be so enjoyable if we set our "unpolite" ways and anger to the side. Let everyone you meet know what a great catch you are and how fun you can make an evening, or afternoon, or morning or all three if you're on a roll!

Invisible B.S.

1. Figure out what it is you want to get out of Internet dating *before* you get started.
2. Try to make your intentions as clear as you can when seeking someone out. Trying to match up someone looking strictly for a physical/intimate relationship with someone looking for a pen pal is the proverbial "oil and water."
3. If you're looking for someone to talk to, which is what some people only want, go to online chat rooms, *anywhere* but the matchmaker sites.
4. If you make plans to get together and decide not to go, if you don't have the balls to call and cancel, at least forward an email, and please, preferably more than ten minutes before your scheduled date. You're a better person for doing so.
5. If you're afraid to meet because you don't know if people will like you, do whatever you can to build up your self-confidence. Change is good.
6. With Internet dating, getting "stood up" can mean email communication stopping without explanation, someone saying they will call to set up a time to meet and never do, or actually setting up a date, but failing to show up.

7. The best way of dealing with the above-mentioned situations is to GET OVER IT! Even though it is extremely inconsiderate and rude, trying to figure out why someone didn't respond is only going to drive you nuts. Chalk it up as their loss and move on.

"I'm still holding out for my 100% perfect soul mate, and I *won't* settle for anything less!"

15 Ollie-Ollie-Ox-In-Free

Why It Is Difficult Meeting People

I know that we were all put on this planet for no other reason than to find our perfect soul mate so we can live happily ever after. Right? Well, maybe that's the case for all you diehards who read those lovely little romance novels.

Why is it so difficult to find a person we enjoy being with for more than three dates? I mean there are road maps to help us find our destinations, (I think you guys remember what those are now, don't you?) there are, or I should say used to be, encyclopedias to help us find information on everything from Aardvarks to Zygotes, and they have yellow pages to help us locate people and businesses. So now that we have total access to the World Wide Web, which serves to hook us up with the "Whole Wide World," then why is it still a pain for some to find a perfect match?

Did you catch that last sentence? Perfect match? Yeah, that one. I think that's what's throwing us all off course. Everyone seems to be looking for the "perfect" match. According to my *Random House Dictionary*, the definition for perfect is: 1) having all the desired qualities, 2) having no flaws or shortcomings, and 3) correct in every detail.

Has anyone *ever* found anyone that fits the above description? I don't think so. I think we all *think* we're perfect, and I think we all *think* we will find our perfect match, but here's a newsflash for ya, "We're not perfect!" And neither is anyone else on this planet. So why are we continuing to search for eons looking for something that doesn't exist? If you should happen to locate someone who is perfect, he or she will probably have a big oval head, slanted black eyes and a green skinny body. So give it up, will ya!

I saw this ad where the guy's headline was "The Girl I'm Looking For Doesn't Exit." Let me ponder this for a moment. Okay, he is a very honest man, and his statement is fairly accurate, so if he feels this way why is he bothering to look for her?

Now that we have every available resource at our fingertips, what's our excuse now? Why are so many people dissatisfied with who they meet? Why can't some of us get past the first date? Well, we're too damn picky for one. We want our fairy tale romance, we want to have our cake and eat it too, we want our pie and the al a mode, we want extra this, super-sized that, we want it all.

I have seen so many ads where guys and gals say they are "looking for perfection and will settle for nothing less." Like I say, go down the road, turn left at the first stop sign, continue on until you hit the next galaxy and keep going until the universe dead ends. Jiminy petes.

I read ad after ad after ad that say, "I want someone who is tall, slender, educated, makes a million bucks, looks like a million bucks, worldly, scintillating, gorgeous, sexy, and knows how to cook." And of course everyone wants that delightful sense of humor as well, probably more so than wanting someone with double D's or someone who drives a Ferrari. (Yeah, right.)

I know I have mentioned looks a zillion times because unfortunately, that is the number one "item" on the menu, at least for the men, and don't you *even* think about denying it. I have had guys tell me I sound perfect, I have all the qualities they are looking for and are extremely anxious to meet, that is *before* I send a photo. After one is sent, I may hear nothing back for the rest of my life, sometimes even longer. (Hey, I may not have the looks of a runway model, but I often have guys shoot me the "up and down look.") Sure, they say beauty is only skin deep—well, in this case, it isn't even a Kodachrome layer thick! What happened to all the "You sound like someone I could spend the rest of my life with" stuff? How shallow.

But to be fair, many of us women have the same syndrome going. We want Brad Pitt with Donald Trump's income, strong and macho, but sensitive, and oh yeah, totally devoted to us. So, you will settle for nothing less than perfection, huh? Don't you realize that hanging on to a fantasy of perfection will keep you moving from one date to the next and never finding what you want, because perfection simply doesn't exist on this planet? Excellence, however, is all around. We just can't see it because we are blinded by our own illusions.

Why not take a gamble and go out with someone who has one or two less qualities than what's on your list? When you meet someone, listen to what they have to say, then look deep into his or her eyes and see what you might find. You may be surprised. Focus on the twenty positive traits you see versus the *one* negative trait. So what if she turns out to weigh fifteen pounds more than you expected or he has more hair on his back than on his head. Grow up Junior and Juniorettes and get over it. What do you have to lose but one lonely night by yourself? Besides that, if it doesn't work out, he or she could have tons of cute friends.

Try something daring and go out with someone you have never seen a picture of. I have done this many times. As a matter of fact when I first started Internet dating photos weren't even included. I met everybody based on how they described themselves. Scary, huh? In a way I think it was better because you didn't go with such high expectations only to be disappointed after you met. Before I would meet the guy I would picture some short, 4'9", 250-pound guy with rotten teeth and orange hair, and then no matter what he looked liked, I was usually pleasantly surprised.

Speaking of the olden days, do you remember what was out there before "photoless" Internet ads? Newspaper personal ads. People would go through the newspaper to find a date the same way you went through the want ads to find a used car or "pre-owned" furniture. I thought, hey, I've found cheap, used things in the want ads before, why not look there for the person I want to marry and grow old with.

Gee, you think it's tough building up the courage to respond to ads on the Internet, which have up to five pages of info and pictures, try mustering up the courage to answer a rather short, usually 20 to 30 words in length, nondescriptive ad that said next to nothing about this person or what they were looking for. To give you an example, a typical newspaper ad from a male would read something like:

> "Single white male, 5'11", 175 lbs., mid 30's, attractive, athletic and successful, seeks single, attractive female, 30's, who enjoys movies, dining out and walks in the park."

Translation: "Single white horny male, mid 40's, slightly better looking than most guys down at the bowling alley, has a gym membership but hasn't seen the inside of it since high school, has finally tackled a full time job, seeks Playboy model, age 18-24, who enjoys renting videos, cooking my dinner, and a good romp in the hay before she goes home for the evening."

An ad from a female may have read something like:

> "Single attractive female, 24, 5'5", blonde hair, great personality, family oriented, seeks single attractive male, successful, athletic, who enjoys movies, dining out, walks on the beach and intimate conversation."
>
> Translation: "Recently divorced, (if I was real attractive would I be putting an ad in the newspaper?), 44, 6', weight excluded (for obvious reasons) because I am sure you will learn to love me for who I am inside. I have a great personality, I am only taking two antidepressants now, I have four kids from three different dads; seeks Tom Cruise look-a-like who makes enough money so I can quit my job, who will be a good daddy to my adorable little hellions, and who is willing to wear a ball and chain and do as I say 'til death us do part."

Short, little ads were all that we had to go on back then and surprisingly, meeting people this way actually worked on occasion. I know it did in one case. That's how I met *my* husband, okay, my "ex" husband. Whatever. To this day, I don't think many of our friends and family knew exactly how we met, and of course that's always the first question people would ask. We told everyone we met at a "tavern," (not a bar), which is where we met on our first date, so it wasn't really lying, was it? I think my husband was somewhat uncomfortable with the idea of how we met and basically shared it with no one. All I can say is if no one knew how we met back then they all do now!

My point of bringing up ancient history is to let you know that we were able to meet people with fewer resources and less information and shorter geographic regions, and now that we have more than we can handle, we still can't seem to find anyone. Could that be the problem now, we've gone from famine to feast? Do we have *too* many choices now?

Some people scan through ads so quickly, they don't even spend any time digesting what they read in each ad because they are so anxious to see the next one and the one after that, and so on and so on. They dare not spend *too* much time with one because there might be someone better around the cyber-corner. Then they usually make a decision to delete an ad based on that one little photo, sadly overlooking the precious "innards" of who a person is, you know that entire written section of the ad people spend a lot of time and energy filling out to describe themselves and their every want and need.

There's an endless supply of people to chose from now, that is unless you live in certain places like Antarctica or rural Montana where the population is sparse. The numbers may not be super high, but you still have the capability of being in contact with anyone anywhere.

So you go out with someone and you don't like the way she fixes her hair, or you don't like the way he talks to waiters, or his car isn't fancy enough, or you don't like how she dresses, you know you can drop them off at their house, go home, and start looking for someone new that night. I like to call this phenomenon, "Disposable Dating."

Like I mentioned earlier, when there were fewer people to choose from, you had the tendency of hanging around someone longer. The more time you spent together the more you learned and the closer you would grow. I do believe in love at first sight, but statistically, I feel the majority of people fall in love over a period of time. That or the guy gets so used to the woman cooking, cleaning, and doing his laundry that he doesn't *want* to lose the perks.

But all that has changed now. Too often we don't even give a person a second chance to get to know each other. People are totally into this chemistry notion, they feel if sparks aren't flying in the first ten minutes, why waste your time. In my twenty years of dating, I saw sparks fly one time in the first ten minutes, ONE time. The minute our eyes met, I felt a surge of electricity only Ted Bundy would know more about.

Anyhow, it's something that doesn't happen too often, folks, so why not see if sparks fly on the third date or maybe the fourth date. That is, if the person seems fairly normal. If there's nothing funky going on, and they don't look like someone out of a horror flick, and they aren't completely self-indulgent, give it the old college try one more time.

To make matters even worse, not only do some people sign up for one matchmaker site, they sign up for three or four or ten in hopes of upping the odds of meeting the perfect soul mate. Again, we all know it's a numbers game. And it's even a bigger numbers game when you live in a big city, like Los Angeles, New York, or Chicago. There are so many ads posted it can literally make your head spin. It was very stimulating in the beginning because it was all new and exciting, but after a while it can become overwhelming, and sometimes even depressing.

You post an ad then all of a sudden you can be inundated with responses, there are so many to answer you don't know where to begin. One day you have no one to go out with then the next you have dozens. So where *do* you begin? I guess you can start with the process of elimination.

I'm going to guess the first ads women delete are the guys who put down their real income of $25,000 a year. Then you delete the ones that live out of state, the ones that are too short or too heavy or the ones without hair or the ones who have too many kids or whatever. The sad thing is the ads that win out for the women are usually the guys with the largest income brackets, and the women's ads with the most attractive photos for the men. Am I on target here?

This is not, I repeat NOT the case for everyone, so don't start firing off angry defensive letters. It *is*, unfortunately, a reality for many, if not most.

Women usually do have a tendency of receiving more responses than men. Why? One, they usually put up better photos, and two, there are way more men Internet dating than there are women. I have heard a ratio for online dating of 10 men for every one woman. Sounds like a good number, but then again, I've heard that 52.4% of all statistics are made up on the spot, so what is the real truth?

In the beginning, when I was trying to find *my* perfect match, I was just *answering* the guys' ads. I thought I could be more selective that way. But when *that* plan wasn't working, I decided to post my own ad. I literally got hundreds of replies within a two-month period. Now I'm not bragging, okay maybe a little, but remember I'm in a "town" of eleven million people. Makes that number seem a little less significant now, doesn't it? Anyhow, since few guys responded back from the ads I answered, I assumed I would only get a dozen or so responses from my ad and that would be all.

It was great at first, kind of like my birthday coming early. I definitely felt the ego boost and the self-esteem soar. I couldn't believe all the wonderful things these guys were saying, I walked around with my head in the clouds for weeks. There is absolutely no better feeling than to receive compliments. I definitely could see where people can get used to this.

But after a while I felt completely overwhelmed. My joy turned to confusion; I didn't even have time to write, that is, type back to most of them. Then I started getting second letters asking why I haven't responded to their first letter. Jeepers, I didn't know what to say. "Gee, you're 287th on the list. Sit back, read a book, or two, hold on to your horses and I will contact you when your number comes up."

I felt bad because there was definitely a husband in that batch somewhere, but I had to let 95 percent of them go. I contacted maybe fifteen or twenty and only met seven or eight. There was only a few that lasted more than two dates, none lasted more than four. I was so overwhelmed I couldn't begin narrowing down my choices so I just sadly deleted them.

I think—and this is just my humble opinion based on my years of experience—if you are truly looking to meet someone online for a long-term relationship, you need to cut back on a few things. Start by signing up with just one dating service and limit yourself to a one month membership. (Gee, I just got the support of all Internet dating services with that one, didn't I?) Most memberships are set up so that the more months you sign up for, the cheaper it is per month. Gosh, let's go with the five-year package, that way we can save $6.95.

I can see some guy falling for a nice, sweet gal, their relationship blossoms, he loves everything about her, he's starting to make plans for their future, he goes looking for engagement rings, then all of a sudden he remembers he has seven months left on his membership and doesn't want to waste the remaining fifty bucks, so he has to continue his dating quest, he had no other choice, I mean $50 is $50.

If you feel a need to sign up for a dozen matchmaker sites, you may want to rethink what your objective is. Concentrate on less numbers, it could be more beneficial in the long run.

I don't know about you but I see signing up for every service for years on end as a potential problem. No one can *freakin'* commit. It was bad enough in the past, but it's totally impossible today. "Oh my gosh, I love Tommy to death, I can see spending the rest of my life with him, but let me just take *one* last peak and see if I can find someone who may be an inch taller, with an ever-so-slightly better body, or who has a quarter-inch fatter wallet, and if no one else fits this description, Tommy and I will then live happily ever after."

If someone signs up for a year membership, are they truly trying to find someone or are they a pessimist? Or are they just looking to play the field? Limit your membership at first and see what happens. (That is if you want a serious, one on one relationship.)

Big problem here, folks, biiiiiig problem. Do you know what happens when you want just *one* more drink, or when you want just *one* more hit, or when you want to work just *one* more hour, it leads to something called "addiction." I can hear people yelling at me now, "You're crazy, I'm not addicted to this thing, I'll prove it as soon as I finish answering just this *one* last ad."

You may think I'm nuts—or more nuts than you thought before—but I have actually talked to people who used the word "addiction" in their conversation when talking about Internet dating. Looking on the bright side, this new "up and coming" addiction could lead to more employment opportunities. Facilities will have to be opened to treat the "Internet love addict." Then of course we will need counselors, people to man the twenty-four hour "Internet Dating Love Addicted" hotline, and of course we will need someone to print and distribute the t-shirts that read, "I promise not to spend more than one hour Internet dating each day. I promise not to spend more than one hour Internet dating each day. I promise not to spend…"

Yes, I have mentioned more than once the incredible amount of time people spend mate hunting. (You have got to be thankful Internet providers don't charge by the hour anymore.) If you spend more time on the computer than you spend with your friends, your family, and if applicable, your kids combined, I think we can be in agreement that you are, if not already, becoming an Internet dating addict. This is probably the only part I am not making fun of because it can truly lead to harmful side effects.

If you are spending more time in front of the computer, than in front of your family and friends, we have a problem, Houston.

Take this little test: See if you can go all day without checking your email no more than one time. Then see if you can go twenty-four hours without writing an email or responding to any emails. Finally, see if you can go 48 hours without browsing through your matchmaker Web site(s).

Are you even willing to try? And if you did, how was it? If you can't pass at least one of the three steps mentioned, you need to seriously ask yourself, "What in the hell am I doing!" You need to evaluate what your objection is. Do you want to meet a partner or do you want to continue barricading your insecurities behind a piece of equipment?

And finally, if you're intentions are truly wanting to find that perfect mate, there's a couple of questions you may want to ask yourself to determine if the person you are dating is the right one for you. One, "do I have *fun* with this person?" And two, "does he/she make me feel good about myself?" If you come up with two definite "yes!" answers, you are clearly on your way to finding your perfect mate!

So don't miss out on what is happening today in order to have a pipe dream tomorrow. Make Internet dating a *bonus* in your day; don't make it what *makes* your day.

Stubborn B.S.

1. If you're looking for perfection, you are looking up the wrong alley. Start looking for *excellence* instead, there's way more of it out there.

2. Try to limit the number of sites and number of membership months to a minimum. Take your time and don't become overwhelmed with the whole thing.

3. Chemistry doesn't always happen instantly. Give someone a second or third chance to see if anything clicks. The first meeting is usually awkward to begin with.

4. Enjoy the company of whom you are with at the time. Don't be thinking of who's behind matchmaker site number 2.

5. Don't let this piece of equipment enslave you. If you are spending more time on the computer than you are with all the important humans in your life, you may want to reevaluate things a little. (Or a lot!)

6. If the person you're dating makes you feel special, and makes you feel good about yourself, and you have a load of laughs together, he/she may be more right for you than you originally planned!

"No, no. That's only what I did the *first* week of my vacation. Now I'll tell you what I did the second week..."

16 "It's Your Fault!" "No, It's Not, It's Your Fault!"

Reasons Relationships May Not Last

Yes, I realize that there are 10,278 self-help books guiding us through the entire process of how to find a mate, how to relate to the opposite sex, how to communicate with the opposite sex, how to improve our sex lives, how to plan a wedding, how to discipline our kids, how to survive a marriage, and how to survive through divorce. So you're probably thinking you don't need to hear anything more about any of it here. Well, if you feel you *have* heard enough, why isn't every aspect of our relationship peachy and why are all the divorce lawyers up to their greedy little ears in paperwork from thousands of new cases each year involving miserable people who never took the time to read what you need to know about how to make your love life sweet as molasses?

I won't dwell on this issue too much, but since I do have your attention I might as well put my two cents worth in. If you haven't noticed by now, I am pretty straight forward, no beating around any bushes in my approach. I have found that some advice books can drag on and on and on and half the time the book never gets completed because you kept getting sidetracked when the authors would chitter chatter endlessly and you wait patiently as you turn each and every page to see if there is anything significant to know but you don't find the point that you are waiting for them to make so you keep reading and reading and reading then finally *The Drew*

Carey Show comes on and the book gets thrown into a pile of old news papers never to be seen again, so that's why you won't see *me* ramble on forever. Now where was I?

Just to let you know up front, both men *and* women are responsible for the outcome of relationships. Consequently, we need to quit blaming each other for ruining things and we need to look in the mirror and start evaluating what we see.

Do you think there could be any room for improvement? You bet there is. Sometimes I wonder if we subconsciously go out on kamikaze missions to kill any hope of ever having a great mate in our lives. And thanks to the tons of "reality" dating shows, it's making it even harder to strengthen relationships. The entertainment industry, once again, (remember all the little romance movies that *always* have a happy ending where Alphonso *always* ends up with the girl? Geesh, only in the movies!) is creating some very false images of what dating is, could, or should be. How "Einstein-ish" is it to pay some Joe Schmoe a million bucks for selecting a bride on television, only to have the relationship last as long as the next round of commercials. Puh-leeeez.

There's actually a show on television where a woman intrudes into the lives of what appears to be a happy couple and attempts to break them up? Why? Isn't it tough enough to avoid the temptations we face everyday let alone having someone intentionally come in and destroy what took months, if not years to build? And who decided that the word "reality" should be associated with these shows anyhow? If these shows resemble the reality in your life, what the heck kind of surreal life are you living!

More on "Bashing Dating Reality Shows" at 11:00.

It's funny; there are instructions on how to heat a pop tart and instructions on how to put gas in your car, but have we come up with instructions on how to survive living with the opposite sex? Yeah, yeah. Even with the million advice books out there, well, a million and one now, we still have some problem areas. Unfortunately, we are usually past the desperate, lonely, "forced to go to a counselor" stage before we would even consider picking up a book to learn how to fix things.

Relationships are definitely a trial and error thing. And God only knows how many trials have resulted from relationships gone bad. But you're a step above the rest if you have made it this far without ending up in jail or on *The Jerry Springer Show.*

Being a woman, I feel I have a certain amount of license to female bash. I am sorry but I hear and see some of the most pathetic things that women do, that it sometimes makes me want to consider resigning my gender. What are some of you ladies thinking? I definitely am not perfect and I do have my shortcomings but I am floored by stories I hear about some of the stuff women say and do. Let me run some of them by you and see if it rings a familiar bell.

I don't think there is anything more important than how we act on the first date cuz if it doesn't go well, that's it, toots, you are history. You don't have to be on your best behavior and you don't have to pretend to be someone you're not, just be yourself. Guys can sense "plastic" people or phonies a mile away. If you're genuine, friendly, and positive, you're heading in the right direction.

It's really kind of simple, there are only two things you need to be concerned about: body language and what comes out of your mouth. That is, once you get there. I guess the most important thing on a first date is *actually* showing up *and* showing up on time. Guys hate it when women are late and from what I hear, it's a common occurrence. There is nothing like sitting there all alone trying to keep yourself company, wondering if you *are* going to get stood up.

I was over forty-five minutes late on my first date with this one guy. I didn't anticipate it taking *that* long to go 6.2 miles. Traffic was deadlocked and I didn't have his cell phone number. I did leave a message on his home phone, letting him know that I was on my way and please not to think of me as a bad person.

Of course I was completely frustrated by the time I got there and spent the first twenty minutes apologizing. He was just happy I showed up. Wearing that low cut top sure helped take the edge off his mood at that point! Even if you are going to be five minutes late give a courtesy call to put his mind at ease, I know we all have cell phones now so there's no excuse, unless you cross into a dead zone, which is half of most cities. (Can you hear me now?)

Being late is not fashionable like it was years ago. Put yourself in the other person's shoes, wouldn't you like for them to call and let you know that they will be there but just a few minutes late? Have some respect for others.

Okay, finally we are both at the same spot at the same time; let's get back to the second item of importance, conversation.

I don't care if you are a "10½" on the looks scale, what you talk about can cost you big time. Women, including myself, have a tendency to rattle on at times, and talk about things that guys couldn't care less about. I know most women don't want to talk about football, big time wrestling, and monster truck rallies all evening, but try not to get too personal and too "detaily" about your life right away.

One main topic you want to stay away from on your first date is any talk about any "exes" whatsoever. Your date does not need to know how bad the ex-boyfriend or ex-husband treated you. For some reason women must think their new date absolutely can't wait to hear them vent about how bad they were treated by every male on the planet. Besides, if you start talking about all the bad habits your ex-boyfriend had and how he acted like a child and was irresponsible and messy, your new date may get offended. Chances are he has some, if not all, of the same qualities!

Expounding on "exes" all evening is a surefire dampener for guys. Wait awhile for all that stuff.

Most guys really don't need to hear about what idiots they are, so lay low in this area. Guys can sense bitterness a mile away so you may want to leave that at home as well. What does it accomplish anyhow?

Another thing, stop whining and complaining! Do you have any idea how much guys hate whining and complaining? A lot! So put a cork in it. Do you really think they want to hear about your past messed up relationships and miserable life? I guess there might be one or two guys out there who would listen and who might care, but hold off a while, at least until you're married and have a legal contract to bitch.

Whining, complaining, and nagging will surely land you in the recycle bin. Back off a bit!

You may want to squelch the desire to mention what you have accomplished in your last five or six years of therapy as well. Even though it may be Pulitzer Prize winning material, it's probably not his favorite topic. Again, give it some time, like four or five centuries, before bringing it up.

Another tidbit: limit your comments about how bad you think your hair looks, and how heavy the dress makes you look, and how you wish your boobs were bigger and your butt was smaller. Remember, guys are visual. Don't *tell* them which of your body parts you think are too small or too big; if it gets to that in the normal course of events, you'll have an opportunity to let him decide for himself. He may have a whole different (positive) opinion about your anatomy until you give him a new (negative) one. So, let's keep that conversation within our circle of female friends, alrighty?

Remember, guys aren't big on listening to the minutia of your life and find it hard to pay attention for long periods of time. However, if the conversation is along the lines of motorcycles, speedboats or fishing rods, then it's okay to go into detail.

Once you have established a relationship, you can start expressing your self-doubts and concerns more, but let the guy get in the door first. Stuff like the fact you don't like how you look belongs in the negative chitchat category; leave it at home or better yet at the therapist's office. No one likes to be around miserable, depressing, unhappy people. If you feel the need to share, spread it out over the next number of dates in very small doses. Everyone needs to vent and tell about how their day was ruined by a traffic jam or an argument with the boss, or how that psychotic, maniac cop pulled you over just because you decided to cut some slow-moving jerk off with your car because he honked his horn after you gave him the finger. But do keep it to a minimum, okay?

Also, if you have one, keep your low level of self-esteem to yourself. Don't talk about things that bother you, instead of doing something about them. If the dress makes you look big, lose weight. If you don't like your hair, teeth, boobs, or nails do what everyone else does and go out and buy some new ones. Update that old wardrobe and get rid of the types of clothes they wore on "The Brady Bunch." Save the excuses for why you can't or haven't done something about your hang-ups for your grandchildren. People like doers, not dreamers.

Ladies, for your reading pleasure, here is a list of the top ten things to avoid on your first date.

10. Talking about how wonderful you are all evening
9. Taking Midol with your meal
8. Bringing your mother along
7. Talking about how cute the guy is at the next table over
6. Forgetting to tuck the toilet paper far enough into your bra
5. Giving out the number of your favorite therapist
4. Ordering two of the most expensive thing on the menu (one for the road)
3. Making fun of monster truck rallies
2. Asking him for proof of income

And the number one taboo-boo,

1. Talking on the cell phone to your former, current, or future boyfriend.

Come on girls; think about what you're doing. Listen to yourself, and don't forget to listen to the guy occasionally. What is your main mission on this date? It's to land a potential second date, isn't it? Well then start paying attention to what and how much you are saying.

I guess I could have summarized the last number of paragraphs into a few words: be positive and secure, and for Heaven sake, don't NAG. And don't forget about that device we call "humor." You can use it anywhere with anyone on any occasion, unless your date is telling you his dog just died.

In the majority of ads that I read, guys list that a sense of humor is very important. Pay attention here, ladies. Don't you realize that laughter beats out whining and complaining every time? So learn how to laugh, have fun, and for gosh sakes, lighten up.

So now that I've gotten you past the first date, it's important to pay attention to this next section. It can be critical if you are hoping to land a second date with Mr. Wonderful.

I was talking to a friend of mine about her first Internet dating experience. She had an incredible time and told me how well her date and she had connected. They spent hours and hours talking and had the best time. She was on cloud nine. (Especially after the ride they took in his private plane.)

Well, the next day she calls back almost in tears. I couldn't figure out why she was so down after the wonderful date she had earlier. She sounded so depressed, so I'm trying to figure out what could have happened in this short period of time to take her all the way from cloud nine down to the pits of hell?

"I haven't heard from Grant today."

"What? What do you mean you haven't heard from Grant today? That's it? That's what you're hysterical about? Jeepers, I thought somebody died!"

She told me Grant had not emailed her or called her since their date, which was like twelve hours ago. I told her maybe he hadn't got out of bed yet.

She was literally devastated because she hadn't heard back from him in less than twenty-four hours. As a matter of fact *two* days went by and she called to say she *still* had not heard from him. She was freaking out trying to figure out what went wrong. She emailed him like eight times and called leaving messages about perhaps signals getting crossed, and wanting to know what possibly she had done wrong.

Even though she continued to email him for weeks, she and Grant never did go out again. Several months later they did run into each other a few times, (no one got hurt, thank goodness) but that was about it.

Some women go absolutely nuts if they go out with a guy, have a great time and don't hear from him the very next day. They get really aggravated and can't understand why he didn't call. Now, if *two* days pass and no phone call, her rage escalates to a 10.7 on the Richter scale. And mothers, you might as well start looking on the side of milk cartons for your son if he hasn't returned Missy's call within 72 hours.

Hell hath no fury as a woman who has not received a call within 24 hours of her first date. What is up with that? Do you realize that this could be one of the quickest ways to end a relationship that never even got off the ground in the first place? Just because a guy doesn't call you back, you have reason to become homicidal? Then, when he does get a moment to call, you're ready to explode, making Mount St. Helen's blast look like a tiny firecracker, and he has absolutely no idea why.

Things do come up, or maybe he just didn't have anything new to say since he last spoke with you five whole hours ago. Even though guys had a great time, it's usually not in their nature to call immediately and tell you they had a great time. I'm sure this does happen occasionally, but not often. Guys have been known to call up a good buddy to let him know if he got laid, (whether he did or not) but that's probably going to be the extent of it.

Guys, do you realize that women sit next to that phone twenty-four hours a day waiting for your little call? Thank God for cell phones now, at least we can lead a pretty normal life while we wait. Years ago, we held off leaving the house, not running the vacuum (so we wouldn't miss the phone ring) and Heaven help us if we had to use the bathroom.

Ladies, if by chance the guy doesn't call you back, oh let's say in the next two to three days, don't go ballistic, let it go. You don't need to email or send nasty cards wanting to know why he didn't call back. He didn't call back because he didn't want to, or he simply wasn't interested. So what difference does it make *why* he didn't. Do you want to know why he didn't like you so you can change what it was that he didn't like? What if every guy gave a different reason for not wanting to go out again, what would you do, "metamorphosize" yourself into somebody different for each guy you go out with? What? What are you trying to accomplish here?

Just remember that by exploding or becoming irate simply because a guy doesn't call you back probably won't win you the "Miss Congeniality" title. Chill out.

Women seem to have this insatiable need for wanting to know why a guy didn't call or doesn't want to go out again. Drop it. Let it go. All you end up doing is torturing yourself. By emailing and emailing and calling and calling all you do is make yourself look desperate and pitiful. Have a little respect and dignity and simply move on.

Yes, it's very frustrating not hearing back from someone, especially if you had a wonderful time, but sometimes it's best to just put it behind you and look for someone better suited for you and your needs.

Not getting a call within the first twenty-four hours is not a bad thing. Don't get all bent out of shape if the guy doesn't call right away. And when he does call in a few days, try not to lay into him as to why he didn't call sooner. Be glad he called you at all! Remember, patience obtains everything (except tax refund checks). Learn to have patience, and learn how to deal with uncaring people. Now ladies, this is a list of just a few things you do to scare guys away. I will list the other 271 things in my sequel!

I realize that this book is basically about how to improve your Internet dating strategies, but I thought I would add a few more dos and don'ts about dating in general. If you think you have a handle on it, just skip down a few paragraphs.

Let's say you ladies have made it past the first month of dating, and things are going great. Everyone is having a great time, you two guys are bonding, he's happy, you're happy. Want to keep it that way for a while? Then heed my advice here.

Don't EVER use the following words in ANY conversations from here on out, or until you're six feet under, whichever comes first, "Where are we *at* in our relationship," "We need to talk," and "I'm giving you an ultimatum."

Instant relationship death. You *really* must want to land the position of the neighborhood's crazy old cat lady. Is that your dream? I can see, hear *and* feel a guy's gut wrench hundreds of miles away at the very hint of hearing those words. Do you want to know how your relationship is going? Does he keep calling and asking you out time after time after time? Well then, don't you think things are going fine? Be happy. Accept the fact that he enjoys being with you instead of having to have a progress report once a week. Jeepers!

If you feel like you "need to talk," talk. Don't announce that you "need to talk" because you're putting him on the defense immediately. That's probably the *only* position guys don't like to be in, on the defense. They feel like they're getting ready to be attacked. Guys hate getting attacked. So somehow baby step around it.

Now that I have digressed the heck out of this chapter, I would like to hit on another awkward part of a date. I am often confronted with questions about this issue, so I thought I would discuss it briefly.

Your first date is coming to an end, whether you had a great time or a "Ripley would never believe the date I just had" evening, one thing's always for sure. There is a price to pay. The tab. Yep, that check comes either way.

For the past eighteen centuries, it's been protocol that the guy picks up the bill. But now, do we take into consideration this women's lib thing at all? What happens if the woman *asked* the guy out? Would it be the man's responsibility to pay? Even though this can be a perplexing issue, a very common response I get from women is, "Yes, the man should *always* pay."

Most of the females that I have asked about this, say they have *never* paid for a date, at least for the first date. I have, more than once. Is this a bad thing? Numerous guys have told me that I have been the first woman they went out with that even offered to chip in. I know it's tradition, but these are new times we're living in.

Since most women are not in agreement with me on this topic, I'll bet I'm going to get a lot of grief, but is it *always* the man's responsibility to pay the check each and every time?

Unfortunately, there are many women who do go out just for a free ride (giving the rest of us a bad name). And believe it or not men usually know early on in the evening if that's the woman's motive for going out with him.

Money's tight today. Would it hurt to at least offer to chip in (especially since a movie is close to ten bucks now), that is if you want to make a good first impression? I know the advice givers who tell women never to approach men are the same ones who are going to tell you never to pay for a date. Well, if you get plenty of dates and are happy and the guy keeps calling back, great. But if things aren't going quite your way, you may want to consider changing a few things. That is, if you're truly looking for a decent man to be with. There are many women who do, in fact, offer to pay, which I think is great.

There are many guys who will refuse to take a woman's money, but they are very appreciative of the gesture, in and of itself. But even if the man *does* take your money that doesn't mean that he's cheap. He may be allowing you to assert your position that you make good money, too.

Women have told me that if they offer to pay on the first date that the guy will expect it from there on out. If he does, you may want to keep your eyes open to make sure he really isn't a cheapskate!

If this whole money thing is a big problem for you, you can always just meet your dates at a city park and ride on the teeter-totter all day.

I know I haven't mentioned a lot of things that guys do to mess up a date, but I'll just touch on the top two complaints I hear frequently. The first complaint women voice is that the guy seldom asks questions about her and what she likes (I can vouch for this one). Men will go on and on about their lives and don't seem interested in her. And the second one is when a man leaves his manners at home. Don't be afraid you're a weenie or a pussy if you hold the door open for her, or allow her to walk into a room first. Changing these two very simple things can make a night way more enjoyable, guys. So take note.

And now for your enjoyment, to follow are the top ten things for you *guys* to avoid.

10. Meeting your date wearing only a trench coat and sneezing on them the entire night due to a slight draft
9. Forgetting to change out of the black and white striped uniform that has "County Jail" emblazoned on the back
8. Taking Viagra with your meal
7. Checking out the breasts of every woman who walks by
6. Using the drive thru window when taking your date out to eat
5. Checking out the butts of every *man* who walks by
4. Telling your date "after" you just finished your $100 dinner that you left your wallet in your other coat pocket
3. Asking if it would be okay to take your date's mother out
2. Mentioning the fact that Jeffrey Dahmer and Ted Bundy were once your roommates

And the number one thing for guys to avoid on a first date…

1. Telling your date you're in a bad mood because you just had a fight with your wife

Enough B.S.

1. Arrive on time or give a courtesy call if you know you're going to be running late. If you decide to cancel, just call and let them know as well. Standing someone up is the act of a coward.
2. Give a guy a few days to call after the first date; don't get all pouty if he doesn't call back within twenty-four hours.
3. Delete all the nasty letters you were going to send if the guy doesn't return your call or ask you out again. Have a little self-esteem.
4. Refrain from talking about negative stuff on your first few dates.
5. Avoid spending numerous hours and countless brain cells trying to figure out why a guy or gal never called back. Just know it was their loss and move on.
6. Please don't whine, complain, and nag!
7. Chivalry is not necessarily dead. Putting it to good use can win a damsel's heart.

"Married! Whatever gave you the idea that I'm married?"

17 Lying (And Not In the Hortizontal Sense of the Word)

Honesty Is the Best Policy...Right?

Ever since grade school, it was taught that, "Honesty is the Best Policy." While growing up, if us kids were caught lying or cheating, my parents would find the nearest corner to stick us in, or lock us in our room (with no phone, VCR, or Nintendo games). Lying meant punishment.

But as you and I grew up, we had less parental influence, and somewhere down the road, a portion of this dishonest behavior crept into our adult world, but there was no one there to punish us.

So, let me be *brutally* honest here, folks. Would you believe me if I told you that I have *never* once lied in my entire life? Really! Trust me, I would never lie to you.

What, don't you believe me? I can literally *hear* the "yeah right!" comments flying through the computer screen. Well, I would be lying if I told you I never *did* lie, (sorry mom) and *that's* the honest to God's truth.

I don't care what advice I give, what incentives I offer or what monetary advances I might provide, I can't get people to entirely quit lying. It's apparently in our nature. It's such a big part of our lives we probably wouldn't be able to breathe on our own if we didn't lie now and then.

I don't care if you tell the nice policeman who just wrote you a ticket to "Have a nice day!" (when you didn't mean it), or if you tell your best friend you absolutely love her new hairdo, even though you've seen better hairstyles on Amazon tribe women who, by the way, missed their last 867 beauty appointments, or if you tell your boss you love your job more than life itself, you're lying. No way around it. So what's my point here? People lie. And some lies are somehow socially acceptable and some aren't. I think it has to do with whether anyone gets hurt in the end. (Just a little tip. Don't ever lie to the nice police officer. Smile and admit to everything! You have a better chance of driving off with a warning vs. the definite ticket you will get for lying.)

I guess it's no biggie if you tell your boyfriend you don't mind him going away on his fishing trip, when in fact you *do* mind. But when you meet a guy and tell him you have no husband and no kids, when your last family photo sitting on the mantle proves otherwise, then I think we need to talk.

So, let's talk about Internet dating and lying. How many times have you heard it said that people who Internet date aren't honest? Lots, right? Well, I hate to burst your bubble, but it's not the Internet that's doing the lying, folks. Computers are inanimate objects, they don't have brains, but the operators "supposedly" do have brains, regardless of how small and how "unused" they are. Therefore, it's NOT the computer's fault for hooking you up with a guy who forgot to tell you about his pregnant wife, or past criminal record. People who date, regardless of the method, will lie on occasion.

When it comes to online dating, what lie is okay and what lie is not okay? That is a very good question and I am so glad you asked for my opinion. I feel the only time it is okay to lie is when you feel it is necessary for your safety or to protect your anonymity. For example, you may want to keep it a secret that you live in a big mansion over looking the ocean, the tennis court, and the swimming pool, just to make sure your date will grow to like you for who you are and not what you possess. What matters most is that what you are lying about (or purposely withholding) will not affect the trust and faith you want to instill in the person you are trying to build an honest relationship with. Ka-peesh?

If I had to choose three topics that people have a tough time answering honestly, I would have to say age, weight and the "insignificant" marital status. Oh yeah, and maybe income. Right? Let's look at each one.

Age. Are we being a bad person if we say we are 39 when in fact we are actually 42? Let me just ask you, *why* would you put 39 if you are 42? We don't know how old you are, and unless someone is an "expert age guesser" like they have at amusement parks, do you think we are going to sit there and try to guess your correct age? The only thing it does for me is get me thinking, "Well, if he lied about that, what else is he lying about?" Right off the bat, I have reason to be suspicious of other things you say, and this is not a smart way to start a new relationship, whaddaya think?

Why lie about your age? If you say you're 39, and you're really 49, but you look 65, chances are the person may not be interested in you because you "look" about 60. Just be honest for crying out loud! It's just a number.

I have had more guys lie to me about their age than any woman I know. But why? What's two or three years? I don't get upset at the fact that he's older than what he says; I am, however, trying to figure out why he had a problem with telling me the truth. "Oh what's a few years?" they would ask. Well, if it's *not* a big deal, then why in the hell lie about it? Are you following me here, people? Could we be a little *insecure* about getting older? I'll let you all in on a little secret, we're ALL getting older, and at exactly the same pace, so lighten up, will ya?

Weight. Now, someone please tell me why in the world you would tell a guy you are a size eight when you're really a size fourteen? As soon as you squeeze through the door, don't you think he just might notice? Do you really think he's going to assume it's the *dress* that makes you look *a few* pounds overweight? Puh-leeez. You're going to walk in and right away the guy's thinking to himself, "Gee, this woman weighs *125* pounds. Holy cow, what does the other leg weigh?"

Now, it's not just you women who forget to mention the fact that your photo was taken seventy-five pounds ago. Men are just as guilty. Believe it or not, everyone on this planet doesn't have to be a lean mean fighting machine to get a date. If the chemistry is there, then five, ten, or fifty pounds may not make a difference. What does, though, is your attitude about it.

If you are okay with your appearance, great, but if it bothers you, get off your butt and do something about it. Unfortunately, most people are attracted to slender people, and I realize that losing weight is one of the toughest things in the world to do. If you are truly unhappy about who you are and what you look like, now's a good time as any to make some positive changes in your life. So put down the Ding Dong and work with me here!

Don't delete someone because the weight they listed may be a little more than you want to handle. The actual weight is irrelevant. One person who weighs 150 looks entirely different than another one who weighs in at 150. (Keep in mind, too, that breast implants can add four or five pounds!)

Marital status. If you are married or even engaged or living with someone, just let us know. We can deal with it from there. Again, I am not the judge and jury on this topic, but I think it's only fair that if you decide to go outside of your marital contract, at least be up front about it. Give the other person the courtesy of deciding if they are okay with that situation for the time being.

By the way, why are marriage licenses the only license that you *don't* renew each year? I'll bet there would be a lot of people who would vote that you have to renew them every, oh, I don't know, four years. Wouldn't it be nice if we didn't have to renew our driver's license every four years? Or how 'bout never having to renew our fishing license or our business license? I'm just curious. If we *did* have to renew our marriage license, I wonder, what would the test be like?

I have had a surprising number of women ask me for advice on having a "suspicious" beau followed. They want to know, "Should I feel justified in hiring a private investigator if certain things about a guy just don't add up?"

My advice is, if the guy does rouse your suspicion and things don't appear quite right, and you think or "know" he's lying, why would you even want to continue seeing him (especially if you haven't even established a dating relationship)? And why would you want him investigated? Just to confirm your suspicions and prove yourself right? Dump the guy and move on. There's rarely a reason to be suspicious unless they *give* you reason to be suspicious. Save the money you were going to spend on an investigator and buy some new clothes, or better yet, go have an incredibly long, soothing massage.

Income. That's a tough one to prove, but if someone says they make six figures and they live in a cardboard box, even if it's a nice two story one, you may have a few questions you want answered.

Income is a factor some guys like to use to lure women in. I'm sure a lot do make the money they say, but I wouldn't answer an ad based solely on that. I mentioned earlier that there are quite a few people who may not want their potential date to know their financial situation or their status in the community. This is a case where I completely understand and support those who choose not to reveal this information. I am sure most of us want to be loved for *who* we are and not how much we are worth.

Yes, we have all been burned before by people who were less than honest. It's painful, we get angry, sometimes homicidal, but we have to move on and not let that stop us from having a truly honest relationship with someone who does happen to have "Abe Lincoln" qualities (the honesty thing, not the tall, lanky, bearded qualities).

If you have been burned, the best way to retaliate is GET OVER IT! And A.S.A.P.

Just to let you know, you're not alone. I too, have had some experiences with total losers. Let me share this lovely story with you and maybe it'll make you feel better.

"Entrepreneur Seeks Goddess." Mmm, this one looked juicy. Let's see, we have a nice professional photo, he's 6'1", 185 lbs., brown hair, post graduate degree, makes six figures, owns his own business, loves music, travel, sports and fine dining. Not just dining, but "fine" dining. He also mentions that he's brutally honest. Sounds like he may have some class, at least on paper. I was betting we wouldn't be meeting at the Burger Barn. Now that we know a little about him, let's see what he's in the market for.

He's looking for a beautiful, elegant, classy woman who is worldly in travel, wines, music, dining, and who can engage in scintillating conversation. Gee, are we a tad picky or what? Why don't you go down to the local "date" manufacturer, tell them what you want, then pick up your "made to order" mate, cuz that's about the only way you'll get everything that's on your wish list, Bucko. Jeepers!

Well, even with all of his elaborate wants, how could I not answer this ad? I am definitely a woman (that's what my last gynecologist said and she seemed fairly competent), I can be beautiful in a really dimly lit, smoked-filled bar from a distance, and I did travel to Indiana and Iowa once. I know the difference between red and white wines (white zinfandel throws me off occasionally, with it being a little pinkish and all); I have attended enough college classes that I *should* have at least two PhD's, and heaven knows I can talk. I'm think I'm in; let's seal this deal now, baby!

When I would see a great ad like this, I used to wonder if I would be good enough for the guy. Just by flipping through ads, and reading all this terrific stuff about these guys, us women can make the assumption that certain guys won't respond back because they may be "too good" for us. Horse ca-ca! My attitude now is if he responds, great, if not, I have 562 more to choose from. You won't know until you try. That's the beauty of this; it's like a human assembly line. If you find a defective one, just push it aside and wait for the next one to come along.

Never pass up on responding because you think you're not good enough. Be brave little soldier, and be positive! And quit beating up on yourself!

Back to my story. I never know if a guy will respond or not, so after I hit that send key, and patiently wait for a response, I have only my bowl of mint chocolate chip ice cream to keep me company until I hear otherwise.

Bingo! He writes back the next day. Is this cool or what? But now I have to face phase two, emailing him a photo. Whose photo should I send him? Certainly not myself! Hmmm. Maybe I could download and send a shot of Carmen Electra? But sooner or later he may want to meet, so I better find one of me. Unfortunately, my best photo was taken when I was two years old, and chances are, he'll want a more recent one. I guess I can send him the one of me standing in the distance, wearing a ball cap and shades where the picture is a tad out of focus. But that would be fudging on my own advice I frequently give others.

I opted for a head and shoulder photo that was taken a month prior. I was very proud of myself, I waited one entire hour before checking to see if he wrote back. But I needed to be more patient, waiting as each minute turned into more minutes. I decided after waiting by my computer for sixteen hours, I better hit the sack, knowing full well the computer would still be there in the morning.

Two days later he wrote and said he that he wanted to get together. Either his definition of beauty, elegance, and class are different than mine or his lasic surgery went awry. Me, elegant and classy? Heck, I was the biggest jock in high school. I have to admit; I always did a great job of coordinating my t-shirts with my gym shorts, though.

Obviously, none of my insecurity garbage mattered because he seemed anxious to meet. He asked if I was available the next night.

Was I available the next night? I'm not Internet dating for my health; of course I'm available.

Normally I like to play hard to get and make the guy wait, but I didn't want to waste another moment with this one. I tried not to sound too excited over the phone, but I'm sure he probably sensed the drool coming out of my mouth and dripping into the mouthpiece of the phone.

Steve and I met at a nice Irish tavern. The first thing he said was, "Well, you sure look a lot better than your photo." I took that as a compliment and asked if he would father my first child.

Believe it or not, Steve looked exactly like his photo. He even had on the same shirt. He was tall, had a great build, nice smile and more importantly, he was a complete gentleman. He opened the door, let me order first, and picked up the tab. Conversation was great, we had similar viewpoints on many topics and had a lot in common. The entire time I'm thinking, "Is he gay or is he married?" because this is going way too smooth.

The main highlight of the evening was when he got up to go to the men's room. As he walked away from me in those very tight jeans, my jaw hit the table. Unga Bunga! We are talking a world class, "10" butt. I am predominantly a "smile and eyes" girl, but sometimes the rules are meant to be pushed aside and stomped on. I started buying him drinks, not to get him drunk so I could take advantage of him, but to watch him make more trips to the restroom.

I can't believe I'm writing about a guy's butt. Don't worry, mom and dad, you didn't raise a loose, floozy bimbo. Honest. I'm completely sold though, where do I sign? I got reeled in by a butt. Is this necessarily a bad thing?

We went out again, and again, and again. He had me line, sink and hooker, or wait, is it the other way around? At the time I didn't know because I was smitten like a girl with her first high school crush. I was definitely on cloud nine. (Where did this "cloud nine" thing come from, by the way? I've used it ump-teen times in my book and I have no idea why a cloud would tie in with the fact that we're in lust!)

Not only did we continue to see each other, I began working with him. I know that could be relationship disaster, but we never worked side by side and we did manage to keep business business and personal stuff personal. He had an operation involving outside sales, which is undoubtedly one of the toughest jobs in the world. But as long as I could help him out and spend more time with him, why not?

One thing that I noticed over time was that I received no special treatment and he had no mercy on me as an employee. Before I started working for him, I had literally been in bed six weeks with bronchitis. I was horribly sick and couldn't seem to get any better. I don't know if he thought I was milking it or what, but he actually told me, "Only wimps and lowlifes stay in bed. Those who are above the rest and who want to succeed will work through it!" So, I did. I worked through it. My first night of work I couldn't even talk.

I soon came to realize that this same level of compassion followed throughout other aspects of our entire relationship. I guess I should have wondered about what a caring person he was (or wasn't) when he didn't even offer to take me to, or pick me up from, the emergency room at the hospital, knowing I had no friends or family in the area to take me. He reminded me what *cabs* were for. Anyone this disrespectful doesn't deserve to be tossed into the recycle bin, more like the meat grinder, if you ask me!

Steve's mood was so up and down, I didn't know how he would be from one day to the next. He seemed so great (six foot, six figures...). At first I dealt with it, but the way he was treating other employees, and people in general, really started bothering me. The odd thing was, he acted completely different when we were out socially. He always picked up the tab, took me to nice places, and paid outrages prices for incredibly great seats at sporting events.

Thinking back, he did have this one little annoying habit on dates. Wherever we went he had this tendency of looking at other women. I know most, if not all women hate that. Usually, I don't mind. I figure it's standard male behavior to glance up when an attractive woman walks by. But with him, it wasn't so much the glancing, as it was the staring and glaring and looking her up and down until she was completely out of sight that started gnawing away at me.

We went to a hockey play-off game one night (great seats, by the way), and we weren't there five minutes when he couldn't quit talking about the cute 25-year-old blonde I was sitting next to. At first I blamed it on the alcohol, but then, when I realized he hadn't started drinking yet, I blamed it on the fact that he was just a womanizing creepoid.

Up to this point, I made excuse after excuse after excuse for him. My friends would point out these inconsiderate, rude, inhumane things he would do, but good ol' Bev always came to the rescue and explained away why Steve said and did the things he did.

The saying "love is blind" is fairly true but they left off the part that besides blind, love is also stupid, *and* downright pathetic at times. Things got real ugly and I couldn't decide whom to call first, mom and dad, Jerry Springer, or Judge Judy.

In due time, the relationship, both professionally and personally, took a little detour south. I started gathering information from people I met who knew him. Things finally started adding up, and I realized that this relationship, great butt or no, was over.

When I finally started standing up for myself, the more I pulled back, the more he would try to make me happy so I wouldn't leave him. Was it because he loved me so much he couldn't live without me? Ha! It was because I was making him tons of money each month, and he didn't want to lose an employee that was available to him 24/7.

You know, the sad thing is I am not a picky person and I don't set my standards unreasonably high, but there comes a point when a person has to let go and move on. No one is perfect and we all have our little faults. I can deal with someone leaving the toilet seat up, squeezing the toothpaste in the middle, and occasionally belching at the dinner table. What I couldn't do was tolerate some of his "minor" imperfections. Little things (I came to find out later) like his secret little cocaine habit, scamming decent people out of their money, and picking up an occasional hooker was a little more than I could swallow. What happened to the worldly, classy, elegant, scintillating women he was wanting? I guess any hooker that uses a MasterCard machine would, in some guys' eyes, be considered classy. Who the hell knows!

After kicking myself four or five hundred times, I felt it was time to find a new job and a new honey. The story did make for a great Christmas letter, though. It was a close call, but I managed to stay off *The Ricki Lake Show*, *Cops*, and *48 Hours*.

So you ask, how did I turn this little catastrophe into humor? Well, keeping myself out of the nut house made me pleased as punch, and knowing people at the IRS is comforting as well!

I was doing such a good job keeping all of this stuff from my folks, too! They told me when I was little I had better fess up to whatever I did because they would find out one way or the other. Well, they proved themselves right once again.

This is just one example to let you know that everything you read is not necessarily true. This guy did *not* have a graduate degree, he did *not* make six figures, legally anyway, he was *not* the CEO of a big company, and the only traveling he did was when he went walking all over people. I have learned that if anyone ever puts the words "brutally honest" in their ad, I have one thing to say, "Run. Run, Lawrence, run!"

If anyone feels they have to tell you a million times they are being honest, slowly pick up your coat and purse, gently open the door and get the hell out of there! A truly honest person uses their actions, not words for proof.

I have considered myself to be a fairly bright and intelligent person. I have always been a good judge of character but this one slipped by me. It goes to show that you have to keep your guard up. Even though our heart makes the majority of our decisions, let the brain do what it's there for. Don't dwell on this stuff, learn from it and move on.

You people are setting yourselves up to be let down quicker than you can blink by being deceitful. THEN you wonder why you don't get asked out again. Think, people think. Like I said, yes people do lie but we have to ask, what do you *honestly* have to gain by lying? And how exactly would you feel if you found out your date was lying to you?

Ask yourself, how will it benefit you, your date, your future children and future grandchildren by lying about something that's so insignificant? Heck, if you're gonna lie, lie big. Tell him you are really a princess from a far away country called Hyakuknik, and that the royal family had to whisk you out of the country because they found out that the village people were going to sacrifice you to the "Phalange Gods" because you were born with six toes on each foot. (For you people who missed out on anatomy class in school, phalange is the scientific name for your little toesies.)

Yes, I could have written an entire book on stories people have told me about a person lying to them on an Internet date. But since you can hear all about these things on *20/20* and *Unsolved Mysteries*, I won't burden you with a lot of detail.

So before you fill out your personal ad and before you start emailing and calling your future "whatever" ask yourself, is this what you would expect from the person you want to be with? If the lies win out, I suggest going to the site, "Unlucky Lonely Liars Club."

The most important thing you can do is listen to friends and family. They tend to see things objectively and only want to protect your best interests. I guess it's because they see things for what they are and have not been influenced by this thing called love. And pay close attention to your gut instinct! It is there to serve your best interests as well.

In my experience, the closer you are able to get to 100% honesty in all categories, the more you increase your odds of finding your "perfect" match, because that is what you will attract. In Internet dating, like attracts like. If you are not attracting honest people, be honest with yourself: exactly how honest are you being in your profile, the picture you chose, and with the answers you give? As the saying goes, "you can only expect of someone else what you are willing to give." So give a lot, get a lot—that is, give a lot of honesty, and you'll get a lot of honesty back! (Whew! That was heavy!)

Honest B.S.

1. The only time you should "lie" is if you are trying to protect your safety or anonyminity.
2. People will be less concerned if you are a few years older than about the fact that you lied about it. If you are hung up on not giving out your exact age, select a site that gives an age range.
3. Before you go out and spend bucks on a private investigator, if you have suspicions and you can't get the answers you want, dump the jerk.
4. Before you answer questions a little untruthfully, put yourself in your recipient's shoes and see how they would feel.

P.S. And for Heaven sake, let more than just a "butt" reel you in. it's not worth it in the END!

I think it's state law or something that every book has to have a happy ending!

18 Oh Shucks, the End Already?

Is This Really All There Is?

At this point, I hope I have instilled in everyone a feeling of comfort and a lot of fun when it comes to Internet dating. My goal was to make you aware of the great things that can come from dating online. Once you learn how to get started, post an ad, know what to say and what not to say, when and where to meet, select a pur-ty picture, and know how to stay away from all the goobers out there, you'll find ease and enjoyment from your experiences.

Many people are hesitant about trying anything that is new and different. Do you remember when telephone answering machines first came out? I remember people saying, "There's no way I'm going to use one of those silly things, they'll have to call back when I'm home." Or how about the VCR, "Why would I want to use one of those, if I miss "All in the Family," so what? Besides, I probably couldn't figure it out anyhow—I only have a Masters degree in engineering." And the good old drive thru ATM machines. "I'm not going to stick my money into a machine, how do I know where it will go? Heck, I'd rather stand in line at the bank for 45 minutes and deposit my money in person where I *know* the tellers won't make any mistakes."

Technology sure has changed our lives immensely over the years to make our life "easier." (Everything except that blasted VCR. Mine's been blinking 12:00 – 12:00 – 12:00 for two decades now.) Years ago people had kids to help work on the farm; today we need them to help us figure out anything that's electronic!

So has this same lovely technology stuff helped in our pursuit of finding our lifelong partner? You better believe it has. It's not only the best way, besides being very convenient, it's extremely thorough. (I heard five success stories of engagements or marriages from Internet dating in *one* week!) Yes, I made "light" of some bad dating experiences, but what I didn't tell you about were all the good people we have all met and all the good matches that have taken place, thanks to the Internet.

Sadly but true, people don't necessarily want to hear about good things that happen, we want to hear the dirt, the low down, and the "bad" stuff that goes on. How many people watch the news to hear, "Well, there's not one traffic accident to report today, Dan, everything's flowing smoothly. No one was killed anywhere in the entire country. Everything's nice and quiet tonight; most of the gang members have been staying home watching "The Art of Creative Tattooing" on the Discovery Channel, so no violence tonight. In the sports arena, it was peaceful at the hockey game this evening, Dan. All the players got along great, and hugs and handshakes replaced the nasty fights that usually occur. Well, that's it for tonight. Thanks and have an uneventful evening."

Boy, with that kind of report, their ratings would probably dive lower than Jacques Cousteau has ever been!

Catch my drift? Booorrrrring. Anyhow, I have met some wonderful guys over the Internet and still maintain friendships with a number of them, even the guy with the gorgeous body I mentioned earlier. Again, many marriages have resulted from meeting online which wouldn't have been possible any other way. Friendships, new golf or tennis partners, and horseback riding partners have been formed, and yes, even our wonderful little annoying Pen Pal people have been united.

I know we have all experienced or heard of a few unhappy and sometimes "nightmarish" experiences with the Internet, but who hasn't had unlucky experiences *before* the Internet came into existence? Remember, the computer is *not* responsible for what happens *after* you meet, that's entirely up to you folks. I know this is a new toy for a lot of you and you're going to want to play for a while. It's your choice if you want to play the field for a short time (or forever), or if you want to look for the perfect "I do" partner right away, whatever makes you happy.

They say that, "Variety *is* the spice of life." (My ex always wanted to know who "they" were. Whenever I would say, "Gee, I heard on the radio that *they* are doing a new study on the effects of agoraphobia and claustrophobia in test tube babies," he would come back and ask, "Who are 'they'?") Anyhow, where the hell was I? Ahh, variety can be the spice of life, at least for a while, but when you start shouting out the wrong name a few times, you may want to opt for the one-on-one thing until you can master more than one person at a time.

You basically get out of Internet dating what you put into it. If you seriously want to find "your perfect soul mate," learn the rules of the game and you'll discover how smoothly things will go. Things can get somewhat hairy if you don't follow the guidelines. Take this young lady for instance:

Jill had put in her ad that she was looking for a serious, committed relationship. Among all of her qualities that she was looking for in a man, she wrote that *punctuality* was at the top of her list. "If you can't be on time, don't bother showing up." Okay, then. She was so desperate, (that's the only word I can come up with to describe the following scenario) that she actually had six dates in one evening. She would tell bachelor number one to meet at a bar in location "A" at 5:00 p.m. and have bachelor number two meet at a bar in location "B" around the corner at 5:30. This continued every half hour for six dates. A case of extreme dating, mmm. The only thing I see her getting out of this is an extreme headache. What could possibly be her goal? To see how many drinks six guys can buy her in one night? To make it in the *Guinness Book of World Records* for most dates in one evening? It certainly wasn't to spend quality time with a guy to get to find out all about him. How could she concentrate on what was going on with one date when she knew she had to be concerned about making it on time for her next "meeting."

I can hear her now whining to all of her girlfriends about how the Internet doesn't work, and that it was a big waste of *one* evening for her. There is no way she could honestly be looking for a serious relationship with tactics like that.

Upsides, downsides, I know we will eventually find what we are looking for and if we *can't* find someone don't forget that we control some of the reasons this may not be happening. Make changes, update the old wardrobe, try a new hairstyle, get contact lenses or lasic surgery, remove the big ol' mole that's in the middle of your forehead, or start catching up on current events so you will have more interesting things to talk about. All of these things can help boost your self-confidence, if nothing else.

Once we do find someone, it's a whole 'nother story (and a whole 'nother book!) on how to keep the fire hot. I've spent half my life trying to figure out what we need to do to keep things fresh, new, and exciting once you do land a good catch. The only solution I could come up with on how to keep things new and exciting is to trade 'em in every six months! Okay, okay! I'm just trying to keep things light and airy, take it easy!

There's one other little tidbit I would like to pass along. Something that has helped me improve *my* relationships with guys is that I started *thinking and acting* like a guy. What did I have to lose? Think about it. If I leave my clothes on the floor, it won't bother me if he does. If I start playing poker and watching football, I won't mind if he does. AND if I leave the toilet seat up, it sure as hell wouldn't bother me if *he* fell in! So there you have it women, in a nutshell. As far as you men go, I don't know what you could possibly do to figure us women out but if you do come up with something let me know, I'll make you an overnight success!

Two things I do know for sure is that the deeper you are in love with someone, the more issues, hang-ups and complications there are.

And the other thing that's a given is that marriage is the number one reason for divorce.

I certainly hope you don't hesitate to start Internet dating—or get back in the saddle if you've taken a break from it. With a fresh, positive and well-informed new start, I know you are in for some wonderful, exciting times!

The Final B.S.

1. Remember to use good screening techniques.
2. Remember all the tips on safety and security while Internet dating!
3. Use good common sense like you would in any aspect of your life.
4. Just be yourself and portray yourself as you really are.
5. Keep a positive outlook. You get back what you give.
6. Keep your head up, smile, and for Heaven's sake, LAUGH!

Best of luck to all, and to all a good date!

Sorry, there is no appendix in this book.
It was taken out back in '81.

About the Author

If there were such a thing as an "expert dater," **Bev Bacon** would be the closest thing to it. Spending the majority of her adult life dating, in one fashion or the other, she has experienced just about every situation imaginable. Her journey down Lover's Lane started out very bumpy when she learned that the first boy she ever dated turned out to like boys, too. She progressed into dating guys who had live-in girlfriends to being the third angle of a lover's triangle. But throughout her journeys she has learned from every situation and felt an urgency to share her wealth of knowledge about Internet dating with the world. Asked if she has settled into holy matrimony after finding the love of her life on the Internet, she stated that doing so would jeopardize her status as a "professional dater."

Bev spent most of her life in Kettering, Ohio, but recently moved to the Los Angeles area to be closer to a larger number of eligible bachelors.

She graduated from Florida State University with a B.S. degree in Psychology. She later became a deputy sheriff in Dayton, Ohio, a freelance photographer, and has now added "Professional Writer" to her resume.

Bev, a Gemini, is very easy going, likes movies, comedy clubs, and dining out, great conversation next to a warm fire, and loves long walks on the beach.

The End

Order Form

Web site orders: www.bevbacon.com
(Credit cards accepted via Web site)
OR:
Return form with check or money order to:

Slapstick Publications
Post Office Box 1012
Burbank, CA 91507-1012

Name____________________________________

Address____________________________________

____

City, State, Zip______________________________

Email (Optional)______________________________

	No. of copies		
Soft cover book:	______	X $14.95 =	____________
CA Sales tax:			
Inside LA County (8.25%)	______	X $1.23 =	____________
Outside LA County (7.25%)	______	X $1.08 =	____________
Shipping	______	X $4.00 =	____________
Total			$____________

International orders: write bev@bevbacon.com

Notes

Notes

Notes

Notes

Notes

Notes